P9-BHY-322

The Norwegian-American Historical Association

GUNNAR GUNDERSEN, *president*

Board of Publications

TOPICAL STUDIES · VOLUME 1

A VOICE OF PROTEST

Norwegians in American Politics, 1890-1917

JON WEFALD

1971

The Norwegian-American Historical Association

NORTHFIELD, MINNESOTA

To Ruth Ann and Skipp

Preface

I⟨T⟩ ⟨HAS⟩ become apparent in recent years that doctoral dissertations will play an increasingly important role in the editorial program of the association. Because of the brevity of these theses in revised form and their specialized nature, a new category of volumes — Topical Studies — is here being introduced and added to our previous four series of books. I am confident that contributions to it, short in length and long on interpretation, will add a refreshing dimension to our publications. Hopefully, too, they will stimulate a re-examination of long-held views and present a welcome forum for scholarly opinions on a variety of subjects. Manuscripts submitted for consideration will be judged by the same standards as contributions to the other series.

A *Voice of Protest*, the first volume in Topical Studies, originated as a historical dissertation at the University of Michigan and meets the requirements for this new series. In it, Jon Wefald carries to a conclusion what several scholars have noted briefly in recent works — that historically Norwegian Americans have stood consistently left of center in their political outlook and action. In this little book, he argues that immigrants from Norway carried with them to the New World a deeply ingrained feeling for community, based on rural values, and that this concept led them both to challenge exploitive capitalism and to take a vigorous part in reform movements, especially in the Middle West. More specifically, he maintains that the Norwegian Americans, their personal ambitions quite modest, have been uniquely sensitive to the needs of the poor and underprivileged in their midst. Relatively immune to the Horatio Alger success myth, they have been quick to respond to movements aimed at curbing profit-hungry corporations. They have been basically motivated by the dream of a co-operative commonwealth — a dream that has been realized by their kinsmen in the present Norwegian welfare state.

Dr. Wefald documents his thesis by quoting extensively from the Norwegian-American press and by comparing the attitudes of its editors with those of corresponding "Yankee" newspapers imbued with the concepts of social Darwinism and laissez-faire economic thought. More significantly, he examines and interprets the performance of representatives of the immigrant group in local, state, and national public life. He contends, among other things, that their "isolationism" during the First World War should be seen as an element in their opposition to railroad, grain, manufacturing, banking, and other interests that had preyed on the basic producers for decades. His spirited presentation almost certainly will invite further study in the political field.

A member of the department of history in Gustavus Adolphus College, St. Peter, Dr. Wefald is currently serving as commissioner of agriculture for the state of Minnesota.

Jane McCarthy, former production manager of the University of Minnesota Press, designed the Topical Studies series, and Helen Thane Katz of St. Paul furnished editorial assistance.

KENNETH O. BJORK

St. Olaf College

Acknowledgments

MANY people encouraged me in developing this story of Norwegian participation in American politics. Two deserve special thanks: Professors John Higham of the University of Michigan and Kenneth O. Bjork of St. Olaf College. Professor Higham first convinced me of the need for such a study, and Professor Bjork, of the need for publishing it.

For help in gathering materials, I want to thank the staffs of several libraries — those of the University of Michigan, Luther College, Gustavus Adolphus College, the Norwegian-American Historical Association, the Minnesota Historical Society, the South Dakota Historical Society, the State Historical Society of North Dakota, and the State Historical Society of Wisconsin.

The University of Michigan and Gustavus Adolphus College assisted me by providing research grants. I am grateful for the kindness and support of Gustavus Adolphus College in general, and especially of Dr. Doniver Lund, chairman of the history department. Professor Bjork and Helen Thane Katz provided thoughtful editing and rewriting. Finally, to my wife Ruth Ann I owe most of all — for encouragement, counsel, and typing.   JON WEFALD

Contents

A VOICE OF PROTEST

Introduction

Iɴ *The Uprooted,* Oscar Handlin claims that peasant immigrants
spurned radical politics in America. Because of their folk traditions
and culture, they rejected the efforts of American reformers. In *The
Age of Reform,* Richard Hofstadter agrees: the immigrants were
suspicious of the reformer's plea for radical innovations in American
society, and restricted the scope of American progressivism. From
Oscar Handlin's *The Uprooted* to Maldwyn Allen Jones's *American
Immigration,* the description of European immigrants remains the
same — they were political conservatives.

For the Norwegians, however, precisely the opposite was true.
They were unrelentingly progressive, frequently radical. Their politics was uniformly left of center, varying from progressive and radical Republicanism to Populism and socialism. In fact, the Norwegian
Americans stood far enough to the left during the period from the
1890's to World War I to be ranked as one of the most consistently
reform-bent ethnic groups in American history.

Geographical and agricultural conditions were not the main factors affecting Norwegian-American politics. Low farm prices, margin-

al land, one-crop farming, and high interest rates merely sharpened it. Rather, folk culture was the pivotal factor in producing a politics of protest. Whether La Follette Republicans in Wisconsin, radical Republicans in South Dakota, Nonpartisan Leaguers in North Dakota, or Farmer-Laborites in Minnesota, Norwegians shared the old-country heritage.

That folk heritage turned on the spirit of social cohesion and communalism. It stressed the notions of economic self-sufficiency and co-operation. And it included compassion for the have-nots and a concern for the common good. The Norwegian rural culture disavowed both the laissez-faire spirit and social Darwinism. It contradicted the success myth and deplored industrial-capitalistic exploitation of the genuine producers. This led finally to a common goal for the Norwegians — the goal of a co-operative commonwealth.

In a book on rural-urban conflict in Norway, Peter A. Munch underlines the ethos of farm life, the profound sense of community, the organic temperament, the concept of sharing that characterized the rural folk, high and low, freeholder and cotter, who were engaged in a common enterprise. Importantly, feudalism had missed Norway. An authentic aristocracy never evolved. The *bønder* or freeholders had remained defiantly independent through the centuries. The *husmenn* or cotters, who cannot be fairly labeled peasants, had never been submerged in serfdom. In short, the rural community, Munch suggests, emerged as "a firmly knit social system which was the product of a long process of adjustment to the social and ecological situation, where every person, every activity, and every social relationship had its rather unshakable place, rhythm, and form." [1]

During the nineteenth century a Norwegian agrarian movement evolved to check an expanding urban, liberal-capitalistic culture, a culture that loomed as a threat to the old rural community. Increasingly, the farmers pitted their values against those of a more individualistic urban society. The development of this rural movement did not mean that the farmers automatically organized a political party, nor that they immediately proposed legislation to

[1] Peter A. Munch, *A Study of Cultural Change: Rural-Urban Conflicts in Norway*, 33–35 (Oslo, 1956); Karen Larsen, *A History of Norway*, 23 (Princeton, 1948); Halvdan Koht and Sigmund Skard, *The Voice of Norway*, 61–74 (New York, 1944); Carlton C. Qualey, *Norwegian Settlement in the United States*, 11 (Northfield, 1938).

defend their interests. Initially it represented a mood, a spirit of
unity, shared values. But the movement was to spark substantial
cultural, economic, and political changes in Norway.[2]

Many farmers, for example, turned to the program of agricultural
co-operatives. That move required little imagination, little daring,
little experimentation. It meant only implementing on a greater scale
the communal and fraternal values that they had always cherished.
In the days before mass production and the multiplication of industrial workshops in the rural villages, the farmer had been simul-
taneously producer and consumer. He had never needed nor liked
middlemen. His economic perspective had been one of self-sufficiency
and self-containment.

The first co-operatives had appeared in the 1860's. Consumer
co-operatives were the *avant-garde*; by 1870 there were 69. Five
years later the total had ballooned to 260, the number dropping
to 215 during the depression of the 1880's. Yet from 1895 to 1915 they
increased from 235 to 550. The Norwegian farmers, as O.B. Grimley
says, were eager "to do away with the middlemen in the distribution of goods and products, in order to bring the producer and
consumer in direct contact with each other."[3]

Producer co-operatives forged ahead too. By the end of the nineteenth century, farmers had established a host of viable organizations among the milk and creamery, meat, egg, and fish producers.
In the group marketing of milk, Norway became a paradigm for
northern Europe. By the twentieth century, agricultural co-operatives
were an integral part of the social fabric. Even today, Harry Eckstein
argues, "one sees no splendidly individualistic farmers' stands offer-
ing produce directly to passers-by; produce is distributed only
through tight little cooperative arrangements, encouraged and sub-
vened by the government."[4]

While the farmers were zealously supporting the system of agri-

[2] Peter A. Munch, "The Peasant Movement in the Scandinavian Countries,"
in *Democratic Folk Movements in Scandinavia*, 18–23 (Minneapolis, 1951);
Munch, *A Study of Cultural Change*, 5.

[3] John Eric Nordskog, *Social Reform in Norway*, 98 (Los Angeles, 1935);
O. B. Grimley, *The New Norway: A People with the Spirit of Cooperation*, 101
(Oslo, 1937).

[4] Grimley, *The New Norway*, 75–101; Harry Eckstein, *Division and Cohesion in Democracy: A Study of Norway*, 11–13, 106 (Princeton, 1966).

cultural co-operatives, they were also rallying behind political forces that aimed at restraining industrial capitalism and equalizing economic conditions. In fact, they became promoters of the welfare state. The social and economic reform legislation of the late nineteenth and twentieth centuries, as Kenneth Bjork contends, "received its major stimulus from the folk drive inherent in the farmer and labor movements." [5]

Because the Labor party was the most progressive political force in Norway, the rural folk flocked to its support. The farm people became its backbone. The first major political victory of the party came in the rural stretches of the Far North, where there was a concentration of small farmers, cotters, and fishermen. The first Labor government, of 1928, was piloted by a farmer, the one of 1935 by the son of a cotter. Even today many of the important Labor party officials and leaders are sons of farmers, and the countryside remains a bastion of strength for the party. David Rodnick maintains that the Norwegian farmers still "have a populist reaction toward what is considered 'big capitalism' and their attitudes indirectly support the Labor Party program for central planning, controlled prices, nationalization of certain key industries, and various aspects of the welfare state." [6]

The Conservative party, representing the other end of the political spectrum, does not fare well in the countryside. This party is the citadel of free enterprise in Norway; thus the farmers largely eschew it. Proposing a more competitive economic system and a limited state function, it attracts mainly the upper middle class, the shipowners, the factory owners, some white-collar workers, and some landowners. [7]

Many farmers reserve their votes for the Liberals and a tidy bloc patronizes the Farmers' party. Although neither party is committed to a socialistic program, both generally support reasonable social-welfare legislation. And both parties, Rodnick claims, are wrapped up in the supposition "that the best way to obtain votes is to restrict

[5] See Kenneth Bjork, "Historical Background of the Scandinavian Folk Movements," in *Democratic Folk Movements*, 5.
[6] David Rodnick, *The Norwegians: A Study in National Culture*, 73–75, 125–128 (Washington, D.C., 1955); Eckstein, *Division and Cohesion*, 49, 125.
[7] Rodnick, *The Norwegians*, 125–127.

the economic power of the businessmen, who in Norway are considered the traditional opponents of the farmer."[8]

Contemporary Norwegians mirror the folk outlook and countenance communal values. They place a high priority on public projects; they demonstrate great solicitude for the disadvantaged; they tolerate substantial material leveling; they spurn the philosophy of social Darwinism. Hence, as Eckstein concludes, the "present Norwegian welfare state is one of the most highly developed anywhere and has an unusually long past. Indeed, the growth of a humanitarian social service state coincides largely with the growth of modern Norway itself."[9]

It can be said that rural culture played a vital role in shaping the course of modern Norwegian history. The rural communities of Norway were highly cohesive, tightly knit. The farm folk revealed great solicitude for the weaker members of their society. In short, given Norwegian agrarian values and institutions, the existence of the contemporary co-operative commonwealth becomes more understandable.

[8] Rodnick, *The Norwegians*, 126.
[9] Stanley Milgram, "Nationality and Conformity," in *Scientific American*, 205:50 (December, 1961); Eckstein, *Division and Cohesion*, 85–90.

I

A Little Norway

F R O M the arrival in 1825 of a small band of Norwegian immigrants on the sloop "Restauration" to the end of World War I, approximately 760,000 Norwegians migrated to America. This movement originated in the rural hinterland, where the interminable valleys, rugged mountains, and countless fjords surrendered little tillable land. The folk dream was one day to own a successful farm. In the old country this frequently remained only a vision. Yet it could become a reality in America. Given the chance, a multitude of Norwegians, including cotters, agricultural laborers, and freeholders, were glad to swap their old-country station for the promise of the New World.[1]

Many Norwegians, particularly the country people, were irritated by the power and arrogance of the official class. They were exasperated by the formalism of the established church and the aloofness of the clergy. Many were alarmed by the rapid increase in population, from 883,000 to 2,217,971 between 1801 and 1900. The harvests

[1] Einar Haugen, "Norwegian Migration to America," in *Norwegian-American Studies and Records*, 18:10 (1954).

were usually insufficient. In the summer of 1838, for example, the crops failed so badly that there was some threat of starvation. The patches of land were too meager. The people saw taxes increasing. "In the face of such conditions," writes Theodore C. Blegen, "came reports of boundless fertile lands available for settlers in the [American] West. These reports came to the ears of people who may be presumed to have had the Teutonic desire to own land." For the rural folk who were pondering emigration, it was precisely these reports of endless lands that provided, as Carlton C. Qualey suggests, "the final compelling argument." [2]

In the nineteenth century, despite exhortations by many crown officials and the pleas of the clergy, an increasing number of Norwegians thought of America as a cornucopia. The emigration movement commenced when a shipload of passengers arrived in New York in July of 1825. But the main stream of Norwegian immigration began in 1836. Twelve hundred Norwegians entered the gates of America in the four years from 1836 to 1840. Seventeen thousand more came in the 1840's. Thirty-six thousand came in the fifties. From 1860 to 1915, roughly 700,000 left the old country for the New World. By 1920 there were approximately 2,000,000 Norwegians in the United States, first to fifth generation. [3]

The bulk of these immigrants preferred the western Middle West, especially the states of Wisconsin, Minnesota, Iowa, and the Dakotas. From the Fox River country of northern Illinois to the western reaches of the Dakotas, from central Iowa to northern Minnesota, they hewed out what they nostalgically called the "New Norway." Laurence M. Larson remarks: "The area thus delimited will include half a dozen counties in northeastern Illinois, a dozen counties in northern and central Iowa, nearly all of Wisconsin and Minnesota, and the eastern parts of the two Dakotas. . . . Within these boundaries eighty per cent, and possibly more, of all the Norwegians who have come to the United States have found their homes." [4]

The folk dream of one day owning a successful farm became, to

[2] Theodore C. Blegen, *Norwegian Migration to America, 1825–1860*, 158–169 (Northfield, 1931); the quotation is from page 169. See also Qualey, *Norwegian Settlement*, 10–12, especially page 11.

[3] Blegen, *Norwegian Migration, 1825–1860*, 19; Olaf M. Norlie, *History of the Norwegian People in America*, 312 (Minneapolis, 1925).

[4] Laurence M. Larson, *The Changing West and Other Essays*, 69–71 (Northfield, 1937).

many, a reality in America. By 1900, 49.8 per cent of all the first-generation Norwegians in America owned or managed farms. By 1900, 63 per cent of the second generation either owned or managed farms. By 1910, nearly 60 per cent of all Norwegians in America were engaged in farming. Indeed, by the turn of the century there was a larger proportion of Norwegians in agriculture than of any other ethnic group in the country.[5]

In re-creating a social order in the New World, the Norwegians expected to blend the agrarian values and institutions of the native land with the freedoms and abundance of America. They were dazzled by the prospects of possessing and commanding land of their own, a vanishing hope for so many in the old country. They lauded the social and economic opportunities of America and were eager, besides, to share in its more unfettered democracy.

Ole Trovatten, writing from Pleasant Springs, Wisconsin, to relatives in the old country, reported that "fertile fields lie uncultivated in America" and that "Every man here has a large number of pigs and also chickens." Anders B. Lassehaug wrote to inquiring friends that opportunities were copious and land inexpensive in America. He added: "I can tell you that I would not come [back] to Norway to live there even if I were given the *gaard* of Erik Olsen Rockne, my nephew. . . . All young, free, and independent persons should come to America."[6]

Eighty immigrants at Muskego, Wisconsin, took it upon themselves to inform friends and relatives in Norway of conditions in America. Their letter accentuated economic opportunity and political freedom: "We have no expectation of gaining riches; but we live under a liberal government in a fruitful land, where freedom and equality are the rule in religious as in civil matters, and where each of us is at liberty to earn his living practically as he chooses. Such opportunities are more to be desired than riches."[7]

Another new arrival in Wisconsin said emphatically in 1845: "We are well pleased with public administration here. . . . The conduct

[5] Knut Gjerset, *History of the Norwegian People*, 2:605 (New York, 1915); Norlie, *Norwegian People in America*, 312, 347.

[6] Quoted in Blegen, *Norwegian Migration, 1825–1860*, 199–201.

[7] Theodore C. Blegen, ed., *Land of Their Choice: The Immigrants Write Home*, 193 (Minneapolis, 1955).

of officials is, as might be expected in a *truly free* country, obliging, gentle, and polite to everybody, not the aristocratic, haughty, repelling kind of address that I met with on several occasions in my old native country." Reaffirming that same impression, a Norwegian correspondence society in Chicago wrote to the people in Voss in 1848 that "Freedom . . . seems as essential to every citizen of the United States as the air he breathes. It is a part of his life which cannot be compromised nor surrendered, and which is cherished and defended as life itself." [8]

But the folk-life style diverged as well, sometimes sharply, from accepted American ideas and institutions. The Norwegian immigrants were largely unable to grasp the meaning and mood of rugged individualism. They were hostile to competitive capitalism and intent on avoiding sharp competition between friends and neighbors. They were suspicious of middlemen and of corporate business. They opposed the practice of buying land for speculative purposes. They hoped instead to retain the important features of the old-country community, its organic qualities, neighborly relationships, and co-operative spirit. They preferred communal and family self-sufficiency, and desired a highly cohesive and socially harmonious community. [9]

Rural people from one community and district would often sail on the same ship and settle in America as a unit. Blegen says that "there was a natural, indeed an inevitable, tendency for the Norwegians to develop compact settlements — communities of neighbors of like origins. . . . They . . . associated themselves with people who had come out of the very valley, the very *bygd* [*community*], from which they themselves hailed in the old country." Norwegians who came from Gudbrandsdal developed the Coon Prairie settlement in Wisconsin; those from Numedal located at Jefferson Prairie, Wisconsin; people from Sogn dominated Goodhue County in Minnesota; Stavanger folk settled in the Story City area of Iowa. [10]

Moreover, the Norwegians, in building their communities in

[8] Blegen, *Land of Their Choice*, 197, 203.
[9] Munch, *A Study of Cultural Change*, 31–40.
[10] Theodore C. Blegen, *Norwegian Migration to America: The American Transition*, 74–76 (Northfield, 1940). The quotation is from page 75.

America, retained much of the old-country ethic, the organic qualities, the neighborly relationships, the co-operative spirit. They made
an effort to avoid pigeonholing people into social classes. Evon Vogt,
in a sociological study of a "typical" Norwegian settlement in the
upper Middle West, claims that they largely eschewed the "marked
social stratification that is characteristic of the Yankee group." Indeed, while the Norwegians tried to minimize and control social
differentiation in the community, the Yankees eagerly predicated a
clear-cut hierarchy of social classes.[11]

In *Democracy in Jonesville*, W. Lloyd Warner similarly suggests
that the Norwegian-American community minimized social stratification. The Norwegians of Jonesville shunned status and class advancement as an end in themselves. They preferred instead a community that was cohesive and congenial. In addition, they chose to
ignore what they considered the somewhat materialistic values of
the Yankees for other values, disparaging the social stratification and
blatant commercialism of their American neighbors.[12]

The Jonesville Norwegians were hardly alone in their judgment
of some native American values and beliefs. One Norwegian immigrant was critical of the business tone set by the Yankee in America.
Writing from Springfield, Illinois, in 1856, illustrating an attitude
shared by many Norwegian Americans, he said: "If a man is a cun-
ning businessman and knows how to get the better of you in a bar-
gain, he is called a Yankee." A letter writer in Faribault, Minnesota,
agreed. The Americans, he observed, "are not satisfied to make such
a poor profit as people do in Norway. There seems almost to be a
silent agreement among all kinds of businessmen here that everybody is to make a good profit on what he has to sell."[13]

From the pen of Olaus Fredrik Duus, a Lutheran pastor in
Waupaca, Wisconsin, came, in 1856, even harsher strictures of
American materialism and anarchy. In the United States, he declared, "there is truly so little honesty and authority that one shud-
ders. I really do not know how long I can endure living under these
beautiful republican conditions where the American God 'Money'

---

[11] See Evon Z. Vogt, Jr., "Social Stratification in the Rural Middlewest: A
Structural Analysis," in *Rural Sociology*, 12:365 (December, 1947).

[12] W. Lloyd Warner, *Democracy in Jonesville: A Study of Quality and Inequality*, 168–192 (New York, 1949).

[13] Blegen, *Land of Their Choice*, 314, 432.

holds the scepter of righteousness and where law and order are held in lowest esteem."[14]

One disillusioned early immigrant, Nikolai Ramm Østgaard, returning to Norway after a sojourn in the New World, jotted down a poem for the benefit of his countrymen. He grieved for the individual who could not maintain the hectic pace of American life, and warned that in America "the way is long for a poor man who must depend upon the charity of others. In Norway no one who begs a lodging for the night is turned away, but a self-made Yankee is less generous: it is everyone for himself over there."[15]

In Johan Bojer's *The Emigrants*, a novel that chronicles the experiences of Norwegians in the Dakotas during the 1880's, Jo Berg expressed the same pathos. Arguing against the theory of survival of the fittest, he said: "As far as he could see across the prairie, he couldn't find a trace of any authorities at all. The State? No doubt it was the duty of the State to give bread to its children. But, however much he strained his eyes, he couldn't see a sign of the State — nothing but the earth, the sky, and himself. Work! Swim or you'll sink: who could make any sense of a cynical law like that?"[16]

Unlike the Yankee, it seems, the Norwegian American was often confused by the compulsive competitiveness found between friends and neighbors in American society. He was not interested in becoming the Natty Bumppo or Horatio Alger hero of the Middle West, pitted ruggedly against nature or his fellow man. Rather he was perfectly at ease on a small farm. Avoiding the world of industrial capitalism, he was usually content with a self-contained homestead. As Leola Bergmann suggests, he did not "have the vision to do things on a grand scale. . . . His is a small-scale life . . . that gets its satisfaction from doing a job well, not demanding spectacular returns for its efforts. Modest in his ambitions for himself, he is also modest in his hopes for his children."

Because the Norwegian American shied away from competitive capitalism and speculative ventures, he seldom entered the arena of big business. He was ordinarily satisfied with his independent

[14] Theodore C. Blegen, ed., *Frontier Parsonage: The Letters of Olaus Fredrik Duus*, 17 (Northfield, 1947).

[15] Theodore C. Blegen and Martin B. Ruud, *Norwegian Emigrant Songs and Ballads*, 221 (Minneapolis, 1936).

[16] Johan Bojer, *The Emigrants*, 100 (New York, 1937).

farm home, his small-town workshop, his general store. When he "acquired a little money in America," concludes Bergmann, "he did not gamble with it, but put it into land or a small store. . . . He had no dreams of power and grandeur. Consequently, his name appears infrequently on the roster of eminent figures in the history of American business."

Some Norwegian-American names, to be sure, did appear on that business roster. There was T. G. Mandt, who produced the famous Stoughton wagon; J. A. Johnson, who founded the Gisholt Machine Company, a corporation that produced turret lathes; Ole Evinrude, who invented and produced Evinrude marine motors; Nelson Olson Nelson, who organized in St. Louis one of the nation's leading building and supply companies. But there were no great Norwegian-American industrial titans.

Nelson Olson Nelson was one of the most interesting Norwegian figures in the world of American industry. He was born in Lillesand in 1844, leaving Norway with his family in 1846 and eventually settling in Missouri. In 1872 he became a bookkeeper for a wholesale hardware and plumbing equipment business in St. Louis. Four years later, at thirty-three, he organized the N. O. Nelson Manufacturing Company.

But Nelson was not a typical American industrialist. He was not a social Darwinist. He was not a believer in the gospel of wealth. He set up a co-operative industry controlled by employees and consumers, and in 1886 introduced a profit-sharing plan. By the end of the 1880's he stopped taking any profits for himself, "being satisfied," as Bergmann states, "with a living wage for his work as manager of his many factories and plants." In 1915 Nelson turned over fifty grocery stores, three meat markets, a condiment factory, a large dairy plant, and a truck farm to his employees. His success in America, Bergmann emphasizes, nevertheless "did not convince Nelson that the industrial system in which he operated was the best of all possible systems." [17]

In a word, the Middle Western Norwegian, in contrast to the Yankee, was little interested in becoming a so-called self-made man.

[17] Material in the preceding five paragraphs is from Leola Nelson Bergmann, *Americans from Norway*, 30, 31, 274–276 (New York, 1950). The quoted material is from pages 31 and 275.

He was not improving his farm for the primary purpose of selling it later for a profit. Like the old-country rural folk, he revered the land, which was central to his existence. As Knut Gjerset has stated, the land held "a certain dignity and worth. . . . It was the pride of the old chieftains; it insured economic well-being and personal independence; it gave stability and permanence to the family in whose possession it remained from century to century. . . . It is worthy of note that this land was held largely for reasons of sentiment, in harmony with the old conception of landownership, rather than as a speculative venture." [18]

While the Norwegian-American tiller of the soil treasured the land and pursued economic self-sufficiency, the native American farmer, according to Joseph Dorfman, was "foot-loose and shifted easily from country to town, interested primarily in the speculative value of land rather than in the farm as a means of livelihood." Richard Hofstadter, too, has explained in *The Age of Reform* that the American farmer was attached only to land values; that he was, in effect, a small businessman on the make; that he was primarily interested in land bargains and a good price. "The characteristic product of American rural society," Hofstadter concludes, "was not a yeoman or a villager, but a harrassed little country businessman who worked very hard, moved all too often, gambled with his land, and made his way alone." [19]

While the Middle Western Norwegian was perfectly at ease on a small farm or content with his small-town general store, the Yankee was often a shrewd, practical trader or businessman, as well as a perceptive contestant in the game of competitive capitalism; he had a gift for speculation, as well as a pride in acquisitiveness; he became ultimately an owner and captain of American industry, as well as a creator of the American dream.[20]

Although old-country rural values, beliefs, and institutions contributed heavily to the shaping of the Norwegian way of life in

[18] See Knut Gjerset, "A Norwegian-American Landnamsman: Ole S. Gjerset," in Norwegian-American Historical Association, *Studies and Records*, 3:94 (1928).

[19] Joseph Dorfman, *Thorstein Veblen and His America*, 7 (New York, 1934); Richard Hofstadter, *The Age of Reform: From Bryan to F. D. R.*, 41–46 (New York, 1955).

[20] William Miller, ed., *Men in Business*, 329–337 (New York, 1952); Carl N. Degler, *Out of Our Past*, 1–8 (New York, 1959).

America, the Lutheran ethic was an important addendum. The doctrine of justification by faith — the historic soul of Lutheranism — furnished a striking contrast to the Calvinistic conception of predestination and "the elect of God." Unlike the exemplary and confident Calvinist who "feels himself to be the destined lord of the world," the diffident Lutheran, as Ernst Troeltsch declares, "takes refuge rather in a purely religious sphere, out of the world." The Calvinist was urged on to intense economic enterprise and success in this world for confirmation of his membership in "the elect." But the Lutheran was held in check, says Troeltsch, by a faith that "never contained an impulse towards a vigorous economic development."[21]

Not all Norwegians in America accepted Lutheranism, and not all looked askance at industrialization. Thorstein Veblen, for one, a descendant of Norwegian rural stock and a great thinker, rejected Lutheranism and hailed industrialization. He enjoyed ridiculing ministers and members of the flock, and approved of the growing mechanization and industrialization in America because of its possibilities for improving productive effort. Because of these predilections, Veblen was generally considered an outsider, a man alienated from his society, *sui generis*.

But Veblen was nevertheless a product of Norwegian-American culture. According to George Frederickson, a good part of his philosophy was merely a systematic analysis and an intellectual articulation of "assumptions which the Norwegian rural community had preserved almost intact for a thousand years." Influenced by the same folk beliefs and assumptions that helped shape the Norwegian-American political mind in the late nineteenth and early twentieth centuries, Veblen came early to criticize the business class of America, to reprove those who were interested only in the speculative value of land, and to abhor the capitalistic notion of producing only for a profit.[22]

Like other Norwegian Americans, Veblen was riled up by "conspicuous consumption" and extreme materialism, and unhappy with "absentee ownership." In his writings, he merely enlarged his con-

---

[21] Ernst Troelstch, *Protestantism and Progress*, 63–82 (Boston, 1958).

[22] George M. Frederickson, "Thorstein Veblen: The Last Viking," in *American Quarterly*, 11:404–409 (Fall, 1959).

cept to include the ownership of industry as well as that of land. Frederickson argues, moreover, that Veblen's belief in "economy as an end in itself, his desire for self-sufficiency of individual producers, and his insistence on 'ownership for use' bear the stamp of *bonde-kultur*. . . . His famous defense of 'workmanship' against 'waste-manship' in society has its origins in the bonde's necessity and desire to make use of all available resources on his homestead." [23]

The Norwegians in the heart land of America did not enter immediately into the ideological politics of state and nation. Rather, they were forced initially to engage in more practical tasks. They were largely preoccupied with their exciting and exhausting errand into the American wilderness. After the wearisome journey across the sea, they had to discover favorable locations for settlement, erect passable dwellings, clear the land, and cultivate crops. They were busy building their own institutions and communities in the Middle West.

[23] Frederickson, in *American Quarterly*, 11:409.

II

Political Involvement

WHEN the Republican party was organized in the 1850's, the Norwegians shifted their political allegiance. They had been Democrats, Free Soilers, even Whigs. The Democratic party had become increasingly identified with slavery and the South; the Free-Soil party was short-lived; and the Whig group had become stereotyped as a hotbed of nativism. The new Republican party, with its slogan of free soil, free speech, and free men, filled a vacuum.[1]

Indeed, after 1865 it seemed almost natural for Norwegian Americans to support the Republican party, which was politically dominant in the agrarian Middle West. It generated an aura of respectability and honor, and radiated an image of everything good and just — a victorious North, abolition, Abraham Lincoln. It ostensibly promoted the general welfare. As Gilbert Haugen, a Republican congressman from Iowa, said in 1904, the party "has never taken a backward step, but has always been the supporting pillar of the

[1] Arlow William Andersen, *The Immigrant Takes His Stand: The Norwegian-American Press and Public Affairs, 1847–1872*, 16–30 (Northfield, 1953); Blegen, *Norwegian Migration: American Transition*, 296–299.

National Government. . . . It has stood for honor, dignity . . . happiness, law, and order."[2]

Religious and ethnic rivalry reinforced Norwegian support for the new party. Virtually from the beginning, Lutherans linked Catholics, especially the Irish Catholics, with the Democratic party. "Anti-Catholic the Norwegian-Americans were," Paul Knaplund writes in his autobiography, "because of their Lutheran upbringing, and anti-Irish they had become because of experiences with Irish foremen on railroad construction crews and in lumber camps."[3]

Even the normally cautious *Skandinaven*, a Norwegian-language paper in Chicago, was caught up in the anti-Irish syndrome. "We cannot forbear thinking," the editor said in April of 1893, "that the country would be just as well off, if fewer offices were held by Irishmen, and more by Norsemen. The Norsemen know how to make, enforce, and obey laws, and that is the sum and substance of good citizenship, clean politics, true statesmanship, and successful state building."[4]

Ethnic rivalry split Norwegian Lutherans and Irish Catholics. But it also divided the Norwegians and the Yankees in local politics. This was revealed by the convention riot at Benson Grove, Iowa, in 1876, described by Laurence M. Larson. The clash occurred over the control of political offices in Winnebago County, in northern Iowa.

The first settlers, mainly native Americans of English, Scotch, and Irish origin, arrived in the Winnebago area in the 1850's. By 1865, the census listed 298 people. During the next five years, however, the Norwegians inundated the county. By the end of the nineteenth century "the population of Winnebago County must have been at least four-fifths Norwegian."

Initially, few Norwegians attained political office. Some suspected that the native Americans "had organized to control offices and other political patronage in the county." Despite the allegation, several Winnebago Norwegians won elections before 1876. In 1867, H. K. Landru was chosen sheriff. A year later, N. K. Landru won the

[2] *Congressional Record*, 38:5262.
[3] Paul Knaplund, *Moorings Old and New: Entries in an Immigrant's Log,* 159 (Madison, Wis., 1963).
[4] *Skandinaven* (Chicago), April 12, 1893. Excerpts from *Skandinaven* are quoted from the English section.

post of register of deeds. In 1869, Peter Lewis succeeded H. K. Landru as sheriff; in 1873, O. T. Severs became county surveyor. Still, native Americans controlled the county's choice political plums, and one of the choicest was the office of treasurer.

That position was held by Judge Robert Clark, a reputable Yankee, from 1867 to 1876, when he died suddenly on August 12. Although another Yankee, W. A. Burnap, was appointed interim treasurer, the Norwegians were prepared to act. "As the voters looked forward to the November election they began to see clearly that the issue was not so much the financial condition of the county as the fate of the old [native-American] organization. The indications were that the Norwegians were preparing to seize control at the courthouse."

A convention to select candidates for county offices was scheduled for October 21 in Benson Grove. The Norwegians challenged the native Americans for every post, from clerk of court to county supervisor. But the decisive test turned on the treasurer's seat. C. D. Smith was the American candidate. Opposing him were two Norwegians, William Larson and Mikkel Peterson.

As the election date approached, tensions mounted. To forestall trouble and possibly to check the Norwegians, it was announced that only judges and other election officials could enter the polling place. The voters had to mark their ballots in the Benson Grove schoolyard and pass them through a schoolhouse window to one of the functionaries.

"It is generally believed," Larson states, "that a 'gang' had been formed to break up the convention if it should appear that the Norwegians were getting the upper hand. At all events, there was a gang, composed mainly of Irishmen and led by the three Bevins brothers, Jim, Frank, and Bill, doughty brawlers who had never been known to refuse a fight."

By late afternoon, a rumor spread that C. D. Smith and his fellows were losing badly to the Norwegians. At four o'clock pandemonium erupted. When Jim Bevins, the husky Irishman, hurled a decayed apple at the Norwegian leader, Hans Peterson, striking him in the eye, the Norwegians and the Irish began to fight.

The riot ended in a draw, but it destroyed the old political organization. With this brawl, the Norwegian farmers were not only antagonized but unified. They won handily the offices of treasurer, sheriff, and supervisor, leaving only those of auditor and superintendent of schools to the native Americans. "By the two elections of 1876 and 1877, the leaders of the immigrant element had come into almost complete control of the county administration, and the same element has kept this control to the present. . . . A Norwegian name long was, and perhaps still is, an asset in the political business of the county."[5]

The Norwegian Americans were scarcely so triumphant everywhere. In Wisconsin's Trempealeau County they never came to dominate the political scene, and ethnic feuds were less conspicuous there. The first inhabitants were primarily Yankees from New England, New York, Pennsylvania, and Ohio. They were soon joined by people from Germany, Scotland, Ireland, England, Norway, Bohemia, and Poland.[6]

Immigrants from Norway won no important county offices from the early 1850's to the late 1870's. But because the Trempealeau Norwegians equaled the number of native Americans by 1870, some political progress was inevitable. In 1876, as Merle Curti says, "the first Norwegian, John Olson Melby . . . appeared on the Republican county slate and was accounted a source of great strength to the ticket." In 1877, a Republican caucus picked two Norwegians, S. E. Listoe and Mathias Anderson, to serve as members of the county convention.[7]

This gesture merely whetted Norwegian appetites. Now they demanded greater representation; in fact, they precipitated a bitter fight in the 1878 Republican convention. Their nominee for sheriff, J. K. Hagestad, was beaten. The Norwegians, undaunted, coaxed Hagestad into running as an independent, and, surprisingly, he won.

This victory paid off. It heightened interest in county politics and it persuaded the Republican leadership to cultivate the Norwegian vote. Indeed, in the 1880 Republican county convention, as Curti explains, "the highest political office at the command of the

[5] The account of the Benson Grove riot is from Larson, *The Changing West*, 39–48.

[6] Merle Curti, *The Making of an American Community: A Case Study of Democracy in a Frontier County*, 84 (Stanford, Calif., 1959).

[7] Curti, *The Making of an American Community*, 96, 104, 326. The quotation is from page 326.

party went, for the first time, to a Norwegian, Peter Ekern, who, with Iver Pederson of Ettrick, stood out among Norwegian spokesmen." Several others, too, were chosen by the convention to run for county office — one for sheriff, another for register of deeds. By 1880, the Norwegians were a powerful force in the politics of Trempealeau County.[8]

Wherever the Norwegians settled — in Wisconsin, Minnesota, Iowa, or the Dakotas — they participated in local public affairs. Their interest in the politics of Iowa's Winnebago County and Wisconsin's Trempealeau County was not unusual: rather, it was typical. In North Dakota's Traill County, in 1889, they commanded three fourths of the best offices, including those of sheriff, treasurer, auditor, and judge of probate. By the turn of the century, they had progressed far in Middle Western county politics. By 1905, according to Juul Dieserud, they had occupied 2,000 county offices.[9]

Although Norwegian Americans engaged in local politics in the 1850's, 1860's, and 1870's in the Middle West, they rarely penetrated state and national politics. They concentrated instead on building houses, farms, workshops, villages, and towns. Their way of life appeared relatively secure, nestled as they were in the agricultural heart land of America. Their interest in politics seemed largely peripheral. To become the town assessor, town clerk, sheriff, or even county treasurer was primarily a matter of local prestige. Personal aspirations, local pride, and an enhanced status for the ethnic group seemed to be the prime considerations in running for a local office.

By the 1880's and 1890's, however, with the culture of an urban, industrial capitalism an increasing threat to the Norwegian way of life, an ideological clash was inevitable. Industrialists and speculators, heading gigantic corporations and financial firms, appeared to be gaining rapidly in political power and influence. By the end of the nineteenth century, the Norwegian farmers, like so many others in the agricultural heart land, were compelled finally to challenge the industrial giants. In 1888 a Willmar, Minnesota, Norwegian expressed their concern in this manner: "We are feeling the effects of their work allready [sic] and when we remember [that] they are

[8] Curti, *The Making of an American Community*, 334.
[9] *Mayville Tribune* (Mayville, N. D.), July 11, 1889; Juul Dieserud, "Norwegians in the Public and Political Life of the United States," in *Scandinavia*, 1:49–58 (March, 1924).

only in their infancy and will make themselves felt more and more as they grow older and get possession of everything in their line we have nothing but the worst to fear." [10]

Knute Nelson, a Norwegian congressman from Minnesota, echoed precisely the same fear. He lashed out at the entire American industrial syndrome — from big banks and corporations to big cities and labor unions. In a speech at Mankato, Minnesota, on June 7, 1887, he maintained that "true wisdom and true statesmanship lie in diffusing rather than in concentrating . . . our labor, capital, manufactures, commerce and traffic. . . . It is possible that large cities may become dangerous monopolies, as well as big railroads and big men." He concluded by suggesting that capitalism needed rigid regulation "and the new order of things based upon firmness and equality, the birthright of every American citizen and community, must take its place. In other words, complete reform involves, to some extent, revolution, regeneration and a new birth." [11]

Skandinaven, too, was aroused by the trend toward monopoly in American business. In November, 1890, it protested: "Combinations are the order of the day. Trusts are today's derangement." The Norwegian Populist governor of South Dakota, Andrew E. Lee, was even more positive in censuring capitalism. "We must get relief from this commercial despotism," he affirmed, "before it secures absolute control of every branch of government. Rich and unscrupulous, enjoying a power to levy unlimited tribute from the public, commanding millions of men who must vote its policies or face starvation, the modern trust run for private profit becomes at once the most collosal [sic] political, as well as social and economic menace the world ever saw. It will destroy the nation unless it is either destroyed or made a servant of the public." [12]

With the surge to power of industrial capitalists in the 1880's and 1890's, Norwegians entered the arena of state and national politics. Now they detested the increasing Yankee political domination and economic power. They would push aside the older politicians —

[10] A. O. Sather to Nils P. Haugen, March 21, 1888, in Nils P. Haugen Papers, State Historical Society of Wisconsin, Madison.

[11] *Daily Pioneer Press* (St. Paul and Minneapolis), June 8, 1887.

[12] *Skandinaven,* November 19, 1890; Andrew E. Lee to Ralph M. Easley, May 25, 1899, in Andrew E. Lee Papers, South Dakota Historical Society, Pierre.

Americans of English, Scottish, Scotch-Irish, and Irish descent. As the president of the Minnesota Viking League declared, the Scandinavians should deliver politically "one tremendous blow . . . to teach the silk stocking, blue blood Yankees that the Scandinavians are not descendents [*sic*] of the lower conditions in nature."[13]

To challenge the Yankees and to unite, the Scandinavians turned to political organization, which became visible by the late 1880's and early 1890's. In Wisconsin and Minnesota, they formed Viking leagues; in the Dakotas and in Iowa, they organized Scandinavian Republican leagues. Their purpose was simple — to concentrate Scandinavian political power, to gain political offices, to win social equality.[14]

A. A. Johnson, writing from West Superior, Wisconsin, to Congressman Nils P. Haugen in 1894, was specific. "I am now in shape to do business," he explained, "since I have allready [*sic*] formed an organization composed of the known Norwegians in politics and are [*sic*] to organize clubs in every ward. It is all secret and a member can not communicate anything on the outside what has been done at the meetings. This is under oath. The organization is to be a Norwegian and Danish Clubb [*sic*] to forward our own people and acquaint them with politics so we can work together and be able to call our people together and control the primaries." In an editorial of October, 1895, *Afholds-Basunen*, a Norwegian-language newspaper, was more general: "Let us move rapidly against bondage and tyranny and let us not hesitate to use politics. . . . Let us read, think, and act for ourselves. Let us consecrate our powers to that which we think is good."[15]

Signs of bitterness among the native Americans surfaced almost everywhere. After a Scandinavian Republican league was formed in North Dakota, the *Mayville Tribune* lashed out hard. E. I. Smith,

[13] See Carl H. Chrislock, "The Politics of Protest in Minnesota, 1890–1901: From Populism to Progressivism," 59, unpublished doctoral dissertation, University of Minnesota, 1954.

[14] *Skandinaven*, May 18, 1898. The purpose of the North Dakota Scandinavian Republican League is explained in *Mayville Tribune*, July 11, 1889.

[15] A. A. Johnson to Haugen, May 14, 1894, in Nils P. Haugen Papers, State Historical Society of Wisconsin, Madison; *Afholds-Basunen* (Hillsboro, N. D.), October 30, 1895. Quotations from Norwegian sources have been translated by the author.

the editor, alleged the league to be "entirely foreign to Americanism and . . . an insult to the honesty — to the intelligence and to the patriotism of that element. . . . The statement made by those fellows at their Fargo Clan-na-Gast, that the Scandinavian element has not been sufficiently recognized in North Dakota is not true." The editor thought the reverse to be the case. "The real facts . . . ," Smith said, "are that the Scandinavian element all over North Dakota today have three-fourths of the best offices in nearly every county. If this be true, where is the discrimination these schemers at Fargo are howling about?" [16]

The *Minneapolis Times*, too, was agitated over the Scandinavian push for political power. Indeed, the editor argued that the Minnesota Republican party was so infiltrated by Scandinavians that no "American need apply, nor any other nationality for that matter. The Scandinavian element in the Republican Party is feeling its oats. It has got the political cinch on the g.o.p. and is going for everything in sight." Equally concerned was the *St. Paul Dispatch*. In fact, George Thompson, the editor, wondered if the "establishment of a Scandinavian state government in this state" was next.[17]

The Norwegians reciprocated. Oliver Anderson of Fargo, North Dakota, charged that the Yankees were conspiring with "corrupt combines" to exclude the Scandinavians from political power. J. W. Johnson of Racine, Wisconsin, accused the former of devising a "Know-Nothing" bloc. Using the example of Martin Johnson, who was narrowly defeated in the North Dakota Republican primary for the United States Senate in 1890, he charged the Yankees with unmitigated discrimination. His evidence included this headline from the *Jamestown Alert*: "COL. ROBINSON WAS THE MAN WHO STARTED THE STAMPEDE THAT TRAMPLED DOWN THE AMBITIOUS ALIEN." He concluded: "In the name of God what excuse can there be for this language in our Republican form of government . . . against the Scandinavian element?" [18]

The innuendoes and contumelies continued. Meanwhile, Nor-

---

[16] *Mayville Tribune*, July 11, 1889.

[17] *Minneapolis Times*, quoted in *Skandinaven*, December 6, 1893; *St. Paul Dispatch*, July 11, 1892.

[18] Oliver Anderson to Jeremiah W. Rusk, January 7, 1890; J. W. Johnson to Nils P. Haugen, January 14, 1890. Both letters are in the Haugen Papers.

wegians scored many key victories in Wisconsin, Minnesota, North Dakota, and South Dakota. From 1880 to 1900, they captured twenty-six important state and national offices. Knute Nelson's triumph in 1882, however, was the turning point. As Laurence M. Larson observes: "The first great political clash between Norse and native leadership came in 1882, when Knute Nelson was put forward as a candidate for Congress in western Minnesota. After a bitter fight the Republican convention divided and two candidates were nominated. The campaign was animated and stirred racial feelings on both sides. Nelson was elected."[19]

Thereafter major victories came thick and fast. Altogether, between 1882 and 1924, Norwegians in Wisconsin, Minnesota, North Dakota, and South Dakota elected five senators, nineteen congressmen, eleven governors, eight lieutenant governors, eight secretaries of state, eleven state treasurers, five state auditors, four attorneys general, and twelve railroad commissioners.[20]

Between 1900 and 1917, Norwegians acquired a substantial number of key political posts in Wisconsin. The governor who succeeded Robert M. La Follette in 1906, James O. Davidson, was Norwegian. The most important member of the state tax commission during Wisconsin's progressive years, according to Robert Maxwell, was a Norwegian, Nils P. Haugen. Three Norwegians became state treasurers during this era — Sewell A. Peterson, James O. Davidson, and Andrew Dahl. Herman Ekern was speaker of the Wisconsin legislative assembly from 1907 to 1911, and state insurance commissioner from 1911 to 1915. Halford Erickson was a member of the railroad commission from 1905 to 1916. One of the foremost progressives in Congress from Wisconsin in this period was a Norwegian, John M. Nelson.[21]

The Norwegians were formidable in Minnesota too. Knute Nelson was United States Senator from 1895 to 1923. Halvor Steenerson and Andrew Volstead, picked in 1903, served in Congress until 1923. For most of these years, the post of state auditor was held by Samuel G. Iverson and J. A. O. Preus. In 1911 Sydney Anderson

[19] Larson, *The Changing West*, 77.
[20] Norlie, *Norwegian People in America*, 485–492.
[21] Robert Maxwell, *La Follette and the Rise of the Progressives in Wisconsin*, 91 (Madison, Wis., 1956); Norlie, *Norwegian People in America*, 489–492.

gained a seat in the national House of Representatives. Carl C. Van Dyke followed in 1915. By 1917, the Norwegians controlled five of the ten Minnesota seats in Congress, one seat in the Senate, the lieutenant governorship, the office of state auditor, and a place on the state railroad commission.[22]

The number of Norwegians in the Minnesota house of representatives reflected clearly their political prominence, especially in a comparison with the Germans, Swedes, and Danes.[23]

PERSONS OF FOREIGN BIRTH OR PARENTAGE
IN MINNESOTA, 1910

	Norwegians	Germans	Swedes	Danes
Percentage . . .	18.8	26.7	18.1	2.5
Number	279,606	396,859	268,018	37,524

MINNESOTA HOUSE OF REPRESENTATIVES

Year	Number	Norwegians	Germans	Swedes	Danes
1893 . . .	115	12	4	8	0
1901 . . .	118	17	8	8	0
1917 . . .	130	21	10	10	2
1931 . . .	131	30	10	14	4

In North Dakota the story was similar. Five Norwegians sat on the railroad commission between 1900 and 1917 — Henry Erickson, John Christianson, Erick Stafne, O. P. N. Anderson, and M. P. Johnson. Three held the office of state treasurer. Two were attorneys general. Asle J. Grønna and Henry T. Helgesen represented North Dakota in Congress, Martin Johnson and, later, Asle J. Grønna in the United States Senate. One was lieutenant governor. By 1917, the Norwegians occupied one of the two United States Senate seats, one of the two Congressional offices, the job of lieutenant governor, the insurance commissionership, and the post of state treasurer.[24]

This predominance was apparent in the North Dakota house of representatives.[25]

[22] Norlie, Norwegian People in America, 489–492.
[23] United States Census, 1910, Population, 2:991; Minnesota, Legislative Manual, 1893, p. 578–596, 1901, p. 680–696, 1917, p. 617–661, 1931, p. 504–534.
[24] Norlie, Norwegian People in America, 489–492.
[25] United States Census, 1910, Population, 3:343; North Dakota, Legislative Manual, 1907, p. 370–381, 1913, p. 522–532, 1919, p. 585–599.

PERSONS OF FOREIGN BIRTH OR PARENTAGE
IN NORTH DAKOTA, 1910

	Norwegians	Germans	Swedes	Danes
Percentage . . .	30.3	14.7	6.6	3.0
Number	123,284	59,767	26,800	12,203

NORTH DAKOTA HOUSE OF REPRESENTATIVES

Year	Number	Norwegians	Germans	Swedes	Danes
1907 . . .	103	30	4	0	1
1913 . . .	103	25	3	4	1
1919 . . .	103	26	4	3	1

Even in South Dakota, Norwegian influence was considerable. Andrew E. Lee was governor from 1897 to 1901, Charles N. Herreid from 1901 to 1905. O. C. Berg became secretary of state in 1901. George C. Johnson was chosen state treasurer in 1909. H. B. Anderson moved into the state auditorship in 1911. Peter Norbeck became South Dakota's third Norwegian governor in 1917.[26]

The South Dakota house of representatives revealed this influence as well.[27]

PERSONS OF FOREIGN BIRTH OR PARENTAGE
IN SOUTH DAKOTA, 1910

	Norwegians	Germans	Swedes	Danes
Percentage . . .	19.1	26.0	7.2	4.7
Number	60,746	82,793	23,292	14,963

SOUTH DAKOTA HOUSE OF REPRESENTATIVES

Year	Number	Norwegians	Germans	Swedes	Danes
1917 . . .	103	22	3	4	1
1925 . . .	103	21	4	7	2

By 1917 Norwegian Americans were an impressive political bloc. They were the most powerful ethnic minority in Wisconsin, Minnesota, North Dakota, and South Dakota. Whether Republicans or agrarian radicals, they were now a force to be reckoned with in the politics of the American Middle West.

[26] Norlie, *Norwegian People in America*, 489–492.
[27] *United States Census*, 1910, *Population*, 3:695; South Dakota, *Legislative Manual*, 1917, p. 644–678, 1925, p. 287–321.

III

Newspaper Response to
American Politics

By the late nineteenth century, the political direction of the Norwegians in the Middle West was set. It was consistently progressive, often radical, and ranged from progressive Republicanism and Populism to Townleyism and socialism. In fact, it stood sufficiently left of center between the eras of Ignatius Donnelly and of Floyd B. Olson to characterize the Norwegians as one of the most consistently reform-minded ethnic groups in America.

They carried reform beliefs with them to the New World. As Elwyn B. Robinson says, "Many Norwegian immigrants had leftist sympathies and were socialists when they came to the Red River Valley; in Norway, socialism was a rural phenomenon." *Skandinaven*, trying to explain why the Norwegians backed Robert M. La Follette in Wisconsin, said essentially the same thing in an editorial of August 1, 1906: "The Norwegians did not march into the La Follette camp; he came into their camp. There is nothing new to Norwegians in the so-called La Follette measures. Effective public control of railroads and other corporations, equal taxation . . . these and other reforms were firmly established in the fatherland of the Norwegians long before La Follette entered public life."[1]

The Norwegian immigrants came from a society where capitalistic exploitation was rigorously curbed — where co-operation, social responsibility, and stability in the community were accented. In this society, as Harry Eckstein suggests, "Communal values . . . are widely shared: caring for public things, solicitude for the weak, and a concomitant willingness to suffer certain private deprivations, including considerable material leveling." The Norwegians came from what was going to become a sophisticated welfare state, where a system of private enterprise is juxtaposed with the equitable distribution of wealth, many genuine public welfare programs, and state ownership of certain key industries.[2]

In North Dakota the Norwegians demonstrated how they transferred old-country values to America. There, according to the census reports of 1910, they formed the largest single ethnic group. As Odd Sverre Løvoll emphasizes in a recent article on the Norwegian press in North Dakota, many Norwegians "had leftist sympathies, and even more of them had few misgivings about pursuing a radical solution to the problems that faced them." In joining the myriad protest movements of the state, the Norwegians revealed the full range of their political left-of-center attitudes — from progressive Republicanism to agrarian radicalism.[3]

A large part of the Norwegian press in North Dakota continued to be identified with the Republican party, which was, after all, the most powerful political organization in the Middle West and had the long-standing loyalty of most Norwegians. That part of the immigrant press, as Løvoll points out, remained "in the left wing of the party and made violent attacks on the conservatives." It battled unflaggingly for sweeping reforms.

Many Norwegian-language papers in the state were even more radical and independent. Some plainly endorsed socialist ideas;

[1] Elwyn B. Robinson, *History of North Dakota*, 329 (Lincoln, Neb., 1966); *Skandinaven*, August 1, 1906.

[2] Harry Eckstein, *Division and Cohesion*, 85–90.

[3] See Odd Sverre Løvoll, "The Norwegian Press in North Dakota," in *Norwegian-American Studies*, 24:78–101 (1970). Quotations from Løvoll in this and the following paragraphs are from pages 81, 86, and 92.

Enderlin Folkeblad, started in 1898, was one. *Fram* of Fargo, a leading Norwegian journal in North Dakota from 1898 to 1917, was another. The editors of two other Fargo papers, *Dakota* (1889–97) and *Dagen* (1897–99), advanced similar views. They, too, "expressed their confidence in the doctrine of state ownership."

Arguing radical theories, a score of Norwegian papers in the state enlisted in the protest movement directed by the Dakota Farmers' Alliance, the Populist party, and the Nonpartisan League. *Fargo Posten* (1885–89), *Vesten* (Fargo, 1888–89), *Dakota-Bladet* (Portland and Hillsboro, 1886–87), and *Afholds-Basunen* (Hillsboro, 1887–96) strongly defended the Farmers' Alliance. *Den Fjerde Juli* (Fargo, 1896–97), *Dakota*, and *Normanden* (Grand Forks, 1887–1954), the latter possibly the most important Norwegian paper ever published in North Dakota, championed the Populist party.

With the formation of the Nonpartisan League in 1915, the two principal journals took opposing positions. While *Fram* evolved into the League's Norwegian mouthpiece, *Normanden* became critical of it. *Normanden* had deserted Populism for the progressive wing of the Republican party in 1893. Its editor wrote: "From a progressive point of view there . . . was no real reason to look upon this movement with displeasure. The only thing about it which might have been viewed with suspicion was the secretive method employed by the paid agents of the organization."[4]

For many North Dakota Norwegians, however, progressive Republicanism was no longer acceptable. In resisting the Nonpartisan League, *Normanden*, as Løvoll explains, "acted against the convictions of many of its subscribers, and hundreds of infuriated Norwegian farmers terminated their subscriptions in protest. They arranged public burnings of the paper. . . . They made the familiar charge that the owners had sold out to reactionary forces bent on keeping the farmers in their place."

In justifying the programs for state ownership of the Nonpartisan League, *Fram* was hardly atypical. Most Norwegian papers in the state seconded this feature of agrarian radicalism. In fact, for virtually a generation the Norwegian-American press all round the

⁴ *Normanden* is quoted in *Mayville Tribune*, March 9, 1916.

Middle West had called for some state ownership schemes and had objected to the iniquities of American industrial capitalism.[5]

Protesting those iniquities, a South Dakota Populist paper, *Fremad*, asked in 1900: "Have the masses of the people the same interests as the capitalists? Are the gains of the capitalists their gain or are the gains of the capitalists their ruin?" Another Populist journal, *Fergus Falls Ugeblad*, declared that oil and coal lands should be nationalized. Singling out John D. Rockefeller and George Baer, *Ugeblad* said that their lands "should be of use for all the people and not just a select few. . . . Rockefeller . . . owns the land where the oil is found but he does not have any more right to it than we do. . . . There is also a man called Baer. . . . He owns the land where the coal is found but really we are the ones who should own it."[6]

Skandinaven, too, was critical of the coal barons, especially because they were trying to boost prices in the winter of 1902–03 by holding back on vital deliveries. Reform of capitalism was imperative. If denied, *Skandinaven* warned, "a mighty popular wave will rise and crush a social system that permits a handful of men to drain the very life-blood of the people. . . . In such a fight the people prize life higher than liberty and if they cannot have both they will establish a social order that will enable the masses to live, whether this order is to be known as state socialism or by any other name."[7]

The Populist *Nye Normanden* was equally indignant. "The many millions of dollars which the coal barons and other speculators now steal from the people is money which they have no moral right to own." With injustices like this, *Nye Normanden* hoped that "the time will come when the people will put themselves in the place of the privileged trust magnates."[8]

The Republican *Syd Dakota Ekko* stressed the effects of industrial capitalism: incredible poverty, negligible concern for the downtrodden, disregard for the public good, and an enormous gap between rich and poor. Asserting that the American "class system is a

[5] Nicolay A. Grevstad to J. A. O. Preus, July 25, 1917, in the Nicolay A. Grevstad Papers, NAHA archives, Northfield.

[6] *Fremad* (Sioux Falls, S. D.), June 14, 1900; *Fergus Falls Ugeblad* (Fergus Falls, Minn.), April 21, 1904.

[7] *Skandinaven*, January 14, 1903.

[8] *Nye Normanden* (Minneapolis), January 6, 13, 1903.

curse," *Ekko* said that on the one side of society live the masters, "on the other side the slaves; on the one side the repressors, on the other side the repressed; on the one side people who live in happiness and joy and on the other side those who suffer because they are lacking the necessary things for livelihood."[9]

To chart the response of the Norwegian-American press in the Middle West to the reform movement during the period of Populism and Progressivism, ten newspapers were studied. They were selected on the basis of political affiliation and location. Of the ten, six were Republican, three were Populist, one was Populist-Prohibitionist. After 1896, three of the Populist journals were Populist-Democratic. Of the ten, three were in North Dakota, three in South Dakota, three in Minnesota, one in Illinois. They represented both urban and rural areas — from Chicago and Minneapolis to Sioux Falls and Hillsboro. In cities like Chicago and Minneapolis, the Norwegians were a small minority. In towns like Sioux Falls and Hillsboro, they comprised a substantial bloc. In the North Dakota counties of Traill and Cass, the home of *Afholds-Basunen* and *Statstidende* (Hillsboro), and *Fram* (Fargo), they constitued the largest ethnic group.

The Middle Western Norwegians, moreover, read newspapers voraciously. One was *Skandinaven*. As Rasmus B. Anderson remarked, the Chicago-based journal "was found in well nigh every Norwegian home in Wisconsin. Its influence in moulding public sentiment among its thousands of readers was simply tremendous." Wherever any number of Norwegians settled, a Norwegian-American newspaper was sure to be. In North Dakota, for example, over fifty were established in the period from 1878 to 1955. By 1910, the total circulation of these papers exceeded 30,000. If subscriptions to out-of-state journals are included, virtually every Norwegian home in North Dakota received at least one Norwegian-language paper. "A final assessment of the Norwegian press in North Dakota," Løvoll suggests, "shows that the papers, especially those in the period up to World War I, were leaders of a regional Norwegian-American community. . . . They guided their readers in pursuing a better life, and gave them a sense of direction and solidarity."[10]

[9] *Syd Dakota Ekko* (Sioux Falls, S. D.), January 11, 1893.
[10] Rasmus B. Anderson, *Life Story of Rasmus B. Anderson*, 617 (Madison, Wis., 1917); Løvoll, in *Norwegian-American Studies*, 24:99.

The better life sought by the Norwegian-American press throughout the western portions of the Middle West involved support for reform — stiff regulation of capitalistic exploitation, an equitable distribution of wealth, the promotion of communal values. It rejected out of hand the dogma of American social Darwinism — self-help, unbridled individualism, and competitive capitalism.

A comparison of native American Republican newspapers with Norwegian-American newspapers in approximately the same cities, towns, and counties makes this common ideology even more visible. While the Norwegians urged a wide-ranging program of reform, the Yankee Republicans pleaded the case for rugged individualism. While Norwegian editors insisted on relief for the poor of America, Yankee editors implored the poverty-stricken to work harder. While the Norwegians backed the demands of American labor, the Yankees condemned workers for excessive radicalism.[11]

The prevailing ideologies of the period — rugged individualism, laissez-faire thinking, and the success myth — were preached repeatedly by the Yankee Republican newspapers. The *Gary Inter-State*, for one, supported them all. Capturing the essence of the American success story, the South Dakota Republican paper editorialized in November of 1892: "It is not the want of money that prevents many from becoming capitalists. It is the way it is thrown away. There is an abundance of money within the power of the working class, money which they might utilize but do not. With frugal habits . . . the well conditioned workmen might in ten years have twenty-five hundred dollars in the bank and combining his savings with twenty others they might have fifty thousand dollars for the purpose of starting any commercial enterprise."[12]

In a later message the editor, J. C. Eakins, blended faith in individual self-help with that of survival of the fittest. "Learn to help yourself," Eakins said, "and you will enjoy perfect independence. Men who can defy adverse circumstances, and can earn a living in any quarter of the world in which they are dropped down . . . are the ones who are really independent." Further, "In the battle of life there is but one way to succeed — fight it out for yourself." To the poor and unemployed he stated: "There are young men who do not

[11] See appendix, p. 87, for newspapers consulted.
[12] *Gary Inter-State* (Gary, S. D.), November 4, 1892.

work, but the world is not proud of them. . . . Nobody likes them; the great busy world doesn't know that they are there."[13]

The ideology of social Darwinism was deeply rooted in the American body politic. But Norwegian-American editors were disbelievers; they blamed society itself for human impoverishment. *Skandinaven*, for example, asserted that there were few genuine opportunities for the underemployed and unemployed in America. Perseverance, self-help, and character development were hardly panaceas for the poverty-stricken. As *Skandinaven* said in 1892, "The opulent often look with contempt upon these people on account of the evidences of filth and degradation about them. . . . But what encouragement is there for thrift and cleanliness amid such surroundings?"[14]

Skandinaven had no faith in the success myth. John D. Rockefeller and Andrew Carnegie had long emphasized individual responsibility and hard work as the keys to success. But one industrial capitalist, Charles M. Schwab of the United States Steel Corporation, was singled out by the paper for perpetuating the Horatio Alger story in America. The editor, Nicolay A. Grevstad, maintained that Schwab's "industry and ability cannot be doubted." Yet, as Grevstad insisted, "the country is full of men who have not been so successful as Mr. Schwab simply because they have not been favored with equal opportunity." Hence, "The truth is that the career of Mr. Schwab is interwoven with the element of . . . 'luck.' His first substantial promotion was due to the accident of a sympathetic voice . . . that fell soft and soothing upon the ears of his chief, the sick steel king, Carnegie. . . . He has instructed young men how to achieve success — permitting them to believe that the instructions were merely the epitomized lessons of his own life."[15]

While *Skandinaven* voiced compassion for the poor, the *Mayville Tribune* labeled the unemployed as tramps. Echoing the ideology of individual self-help, the paper contended: "Tramps become tramps and remain tramps, not because there is anything in our social system that obliges them to be so, but because they are lazy and worthless and . . . choose the pleasures and hardships of tramp life in prefer-

[13] *Gary Inter-State*, April 27, 1893.
[14] *Skandinaven*, February 24, 1892.
[15] *Skandinaven*, January 17, 1902.

ence to the pleasures and hardships of the honest workingmen."
Thus, the "number of persons in the United States who can not make
an honest living — who can not find work at living wages — is very
small — if there are any such."[16]

Fremad, a Populist journal, questioned this judgment. *Fremad*
disparaged industrial America for breeding unemployment. "Most
tramps," said the editor, "are not so from choice. They are out of
work, and in this age when a man gets out of a job and is looking
for another, he is called a tramp."[17]

One theory harped upon by the Yankee press was that of laissez
faire. That doctrine, as the *Drayton Echo* stated, was "better than
looking to the lawmakers for relief. It makes men industrious, self-
reliant, and is a positive gain to civilization." The *Mayville Tribune*
was in full accord: let each individual work out his own problems.
That was the only way, the *Tribune* suggested, because "poverty has
always existed and notwithstanding any and every kind of possible
government or laws it is entirely probable that poverty will forever
continue to be the lot of mankind." Indeed, "The power of the government is powerless to prevent the poverty that proceeds out of
the shortcomings of human nature."[18]

To the *Minneapolis Tribune*, the lessons of history were equally
clear. First, it said, "Personal responsibility and individual risk must
be at the bottom of every theory that is designed to advance civilization and improve the condition of the world at large. When these two
motives are absent trade must stagnate and man degenerate." Second, "The citizen needs less rather than more of governmental control and interference. Let the people manage their own business
affairs for themselves."[19]

This reasoning was inverted by the editors of the Norwegian
newspapers. They refused to accept great wealth as a just reward for
the winners in the game of economic competition. They condemned
the maldistribution of wealth in America and challenged the theory
of noninterference by society.

Many newspapers protested the incredible gap between rich and

[16] *Mayville Tribune*, September 15, 1892.
[17] *Fremad*, December 10, 1896.
[18] *Drayton Echo* (Drayton, N.D.), November 14, 1890; *Mayville Tribune*,
May 24, 1894.
[19] *Minneapolis Tribune*, May 11, 1892.

poor. *Afholds-Basunen* remarked: "For single individuals to get so rich is bad enough, but that so many people are less than rich, if not very poor, is a bad situation indeed." *Syd Dakota Ekko* of Sioux Falls also wondered why the industrial titans were unable to "delineate the differences between having enough and pure greediness." *Statstidende* stated, "It is extremely unhealthy to let single individuals possess such tremendous power and wealth." [20]

Skandinaven scoffed at the law of competition and the doctrine of noninterference. In fact, the editor argued that no industry has a "natural right. It has the community to thank for its existence. When society gives a corporation life, the assumption is that the company should serve and further the public good and not make use of its power to impudently exploit the public. If it misuses its right to live, then society can and should interfere." [21]

Fram of Fargo alleged that the industrial capitalists of America rarely furthered the national welfare. Rather, as *Red River Dalen* (Crookston, Minnesota) asserted, they promoted only their own interests. Using William K. Vanderbilt as an example, *Dalen* said: "If God had from the beginning given Adam an annual salary of $25,000 and allowed him to live until this day, and if Adam had saved every cent of this salary, he would still have been poorer than Wm. Vanderbilt by $50,000,000." *Amerika* of Chicago, agreeing with *Fram* and *Red River Dalen* that the interests of the people and of the owners of industry were diametrically opposed, was offended that the industrial capitalists could "live in joy and abundance on the money which they have pressed out of the poverty of others." The Norwegian editors, in short, were outraged by American capitalism. They were indignant, as the *Syd Dakota Ekko* explained, because the industrial giants "promised us eggs and bread, but they give us stones and scorpions instead." [22]

The Norwegian editors fought for farmers and for rural America, but their greatest fight was for human rights. Falling farm prices

[20] *Afholds-Basunen*, September 3, 1890; *Syd Dakota Ekko*, November 23, 1905; *Statstidende* (Hillsboro, N. D.), April 29, 1902.

[21] *Skandinaven*, February 16, 1900.

[22] *Fram* (Fargo, N.D.), January 24, 1902; editorial from *Red River Dalen* (Crookston, Minn.), quoted in *The North* (Minneapolis), June 15, 1892; *Amerika* (Chicago), quoted in *The North*, September 28, 1892; *Syd Dakota Ekko*, November 22, 1893. *The North* was a newspaper published in English for Scandinavian Americans.

and increasing farm foreclosures were hardly the issue. Rather, it was freedom and human dignity — including freedom and dignity for the workers of America. Here again the Norwegian papers bitterly opposed the capitalist press. While Yankee Republican editors lashed out at strikers and unions, Norwegian editors, even in the smallest towns, were strongly prolabor.

Several of the most violent strikes in American labor history took place in the 1890's. One of the worst occurred at the Homestead plant of the Carnegie Steel Company in Pennsylvania during the summer of 1892. Republican papers like the *Minneapolis Tribune* championed the rights of capital. "The dispute at the Carnegie iron works," the *Tribune* noted, "is so trivial as to make the trouble there and the consequent loss of life which has taken place seem absolutely causeless." Further, the "Tribune insists upon the right of every employer to run his own business without interference from others so long as he keeps within the law."[23]

The *St. Paul Dispatch* denounced the striking Amalgamated Association of Iron and Steel Workers even more strongly: "The doctrines which have been promulgated by the representatives of the Amalgamated societies, concerning the relations of the employers and employes in the Carnegie Steel works, represents a long step away from all the underlying principles of our social and industrial system, and toward the acceptance of the doctrines of socialism and ultimately of anarchy."[24]

Mocking the Homestead strikers and reformers everywhere, the small-town *Dell Rapids Tribune* editorialized in September, 1892: "If reform applies to the wages of the day laborer how can you do more for that class than has already been done? . . . Laborers today are on the rising tide and are better off without reform than with." This same argument applied to the farmers. "So it is with all the farmers through the west. The great majority came here with nothing but their sterling wills and bare hands, and have prospered and grown financially fat."[25]

The *Minneapolis Tribune* reaffirmed its belief in the success myth. Instead of striking, the Homestead workers should set their

[23] *Minneapolis Tribune,* July 7, 1892.
[24] *St. Paul Dispatch,* August 5, 1892.
[25] *Dell Rapids Tribune* (Dell Rapids, S. D.), September 30, 1892.

eyes on loftier goals. "The embarrassing thing about this matter," the *Tribune* said, "is that the workman of today, who sympathizes with the strikers, may be the millionaire of a few years hence in sympathy with the capitalists. There is no knowing when any of us may be hit by a million or two."[26]

The Norwegian-American press, however, contradicted the *Tribune* on the Homestead strike. Kristofer Janson, writing in *Saamanden* of Minneapolis, for example, put it this way: "What has now happened in Pennsylvania involves a serious lesson. We see that capital is not willing . . . to yield to the just demands of labor." *Nordvesten*, although opposed to violence, also defended the strikers. Its sympathies, the St. Paul editor emphasized, "are certainly on the side of the workers because we think that their protest against the reduction of their wages was justified. . . . The workers had a complete right to strike." *Dakota* of Grand Forks and Fargo was disturbed that the Carnegie Steel Company would employ the Pinkerton Detective Agency to break the strike. "Old Rome also had her counterpart of our Pinkerton murderers. The Pretorians were hired and paid by rich private men, bloodsuckers, who had been impoverishing the people so long that they were afraid of the results. . . . The existence of the Pinkerton bandits is a menace to the republic and the liberty of the people, and it is a scandal that it is tolerated in any one of the states of this union."[27]

Statstidende also tilted at the *Minneapolis Tribune*. The Hillsboro weekly remarked that American labor should set its sights on specific goals — a minimum daily wage, a forty-eight-hour work week, and a government pension for all retired workers. Mulling over the Homestead strike and others, *Skandinaven* concluded that "the great majority of the American society sincerely wish that each man and woman in society should have a maximum of rights and justice, that workers everywhere should have a proper and high wage for his labor."[28]

With the panic of 1893, agricultural prices plummeted to new lows, and upwards of a million workers were thrown out of jobs.

[26] *Minneapolis Tribune*, July 9, 1892.
[27] Kristofer Janson, "Arbeidersagen," in *Saamanden*, 6:334 (August, 1892); *Nordvesten* (St. Paul), July 14, 1892; *Dakota* (Grand Forks and Fargo), quoted in *The North*, July 27, 1892.
[28] *Statstidende*, May 25, 1897; *Skandinaven*, July 20, 1892.

For those who were caught up in the depression of the 1890's, Republican papers like the *Gary Inter-State* had an easy solution. As the South Dakota paper argued: "There is no estimating the value of steady, aggressive work. But it is coming. Both capital and labor are being taught a lesson, and the rough and broken sea of business is rocking itself into a calm and ere long the ship of prosperity will have smooth sailing." The *Minneapolis Tribune* suggested that "there is no use in getting excited, no use in getting out of sorts with the world, and worse than folly to go about denouncing 'society' or the government for your condition and demanding of the government work or wages or profits." Finally, "Keep cool. Study the situation. Be charitable in your thoughts, and be sweet." [29]

By contrast, *Skandinaven* was bitter about the depression — bitter that so much poverty and unemployment existed in a land of plenty: "The wheels of industry ceased to revolve. Want knocked at the door of thousands upon thousands of prosperous homes. The ghastly spectre of starvation appeared in the horizon stalking throughout this land which a benign providence made to flow with milk and honey." Immediate and sweeping reforms were required. If these were denied, "It is written that swift vengeance shall overtake men in high places, who moved by perverseness or folly crush the people and grind the faces of the poor, and the workingmen know that in this land of freedom it is their privilege and duty to administer the vengeance and rebuke and punish such rulers." [30]

The *Minneapolis Tribune* scored the Coxey movement as well. It was too radical. The marchers were mere vagabonds. In fact, "Coxey's roving bands of tramps all over the country have been one of labor's greatest enemies. They have driven into quiet places of safety millions of dollars which move the wheels of the world and furnish employment to labor." Labeling the Coxeyites as socialists, the small-town *Faribault Republican* proclaimed the dogma of self-help: "The inspiration of the movement evidently comes from an element of cranks who are of socialistic tendencies and believes that it is the duty of the government to relieve the individual of the responsibility and duty of caring for himself." [31]

[29] *Gary Inter-State*, May 25, 1894; *Minneapolis Tribune*, June 18, 1894.
[30] *Skandinaven*, December 20, 1893.
[31] *Minneapolis Tribune*, June 3, 1894; *Faribault Republican* (Faribault, Minn.), April 25, 1894.

The Pullman strike of 1894 furnished yet another rallying point for the Republican newspapers. The *Rock County Herald*, for one, commented: "Those who . . . uphold the strikers in their acts of violence, are not worthy to enjoy the rights of American citizenship." Further, the strikers "are anarchists, nothing less, and have no place in a free government." For the *St. Paul Pioneer Press*, the issue at stake was nothing less than the rights of capital. The strike "is a war against the rights of property, against the freedom of the citizen, against every man who has a home or is engaged in any kind of business." The *Minneapolis Tribune* blamed "dictatorial strike leaders" for the Pullman stoppage. The *Faribault Republican*, too, claimed that the labor chiefs were only self-seeking demagogues and that the strike was uncalled for. But the Faribault paper had hope for labor — hope that "the truth will dawn upon the great mass of organized laborers, that the interests of capital and labor are identical."[32]

Like the others, the *Faribault Republican* was only uttering the prevailing ideologies of the age. In September, 1900, the *Minneapolis Tribune* put them all together: "During the past few years labor in this country has been remuneratively employed. No competent workman who was willing to work has lacked the opportunity to support himself and his family comfortably." Indeed, "A considerable percentage of the laborers are . . . capitalists, and labor and capital so coincide and run together that it is often hard to tell where one ends and the other begins." Finally, "The highest interest of labor, as of capital, lies in letting well enough alone." The success myth was central to this tale. Every American worker had the opportunity to become a self-made man. As the *Dell Rapids Tribune* concluded: "Nine times in ten, the leading men in the country were originally poor boys."[33]

The Norwegian-American press, however, shelved the success myth and opted for the rights of man. From the Coxey march and the Pullman strike of 1894 to the Pennsylvania mine strike of 1902 and the Chicago tailors' strike of 1910, the Norwegian editors were

[32] *Rock County Herald* (Luverne, Minn.), July 13, 1894; *St. Paul Pioneer Press*, July 1, 1894; *Minneapolis Tribune*, July 28, 1894; *Faribault Republican*, July 11, 1894.
[33] *Minneapolis Tribune*, September 4, 1900; *Dell Rapids Tribune*, October 4, 1901.

strongly prolabor. *Skandinaven* explained, for example, that the incentive for the Coxey march was quite simple. "All they propose to do," the Chicago paper said, "is to appear before Congress and demand work." Further, "It is not amiss to have the present condition of the country brought home to the ponderous knight of crude theories cracking the whip at Washington, and a delegation representing starving workers are the very men to do it." *Nye Normanden* of Minneapolis grumbled that all legal, economic, and political power was on the side of the industrial capitalists. Reminded of the Homestead and Pullman strikes and the defeated Coxey march, *Nye Normanden* stated: "The law, judges, sheriffs, and Winchester rifles are used by the trusts against the workers and in defense of capitalism." [34]

Another Norwegian paper, *Statstidende*, condemned the plethora of industrial sweatshops in America. It impugned the social Darwinism that forced "seamstresses . . . to work for the miserable payment of 40 and 50 cents a day for ten hours of work." *Skandinaven* concurred: "The evils of the 'Sweat Shop' system of work are undeniable. It robs labor of its mankind and self-respect." Cutting down the American ideologies of individualism and competition, *Skandinaven* called the sweat shop system one "under which the faces of the poor are ground by the poor during their struggle with one another for bread — in the quicksands of an excessive and illegitimate competition." Hence, "It should be uprooted at once. The sweat shop must go." [35]

In the first years of the twentieth century, there were several important strikes in Pennsylvania. *Statstidende* backed the miners in the fall of 1900. They "surely have about the hardest work imaginable and yet they are paid meager wages. The miners also have to live in company housing and buy their groceries in company stores." Thus, "It is not surprising . . . that the coal miners would lose their patience and test their power against the coal barons. . . . Let us hope that they have good luck." [36]

Syd Dakota Ekko was particularly concerned with the Pennsylvania coal strikers of 1902. While "those poor fellows suffer," the

[34] *Skandinaven*, August 23, 1893; *Nye Normanden*, October 12, 1897.
[35] *Statstidende*, April 2, 1901; *Skandinaven*, April 1, 1896.
[36] *Statstidende*, September 18, 1900.

Sioux Falls paper declared, "people from all across the land sympathize with the striking workers." *Skandinaven* blasted George F. Baer, president of the Philadelphia and Reading Railroad, for his role in that dispute. Spurning Baer's letter "proclaiming the doctrine of the divine right of the coal owners," the journal asserted that "the 'divine right' of . . . Coal Baron Baer shared a similar fate at the hands of President Roosevelt, John Mitchell, and an army of heroic work people."[37]

For *Fram*, the central issue of the 1902 strikes was human dignity. Strikes were necessary to humanize the system of American industrial capitalism, which too often bred precisely the opposite — poverty, malnutrition, disease, sweatshops, unemployment, degradation. It allowed the capitalists to "pay more attention to the factory mules than they do to the workmen . . . because the mules cost a great deal of money and the workers cost nothing." And too often, as *Fergus Falls Ugeblad* seconded, it forced unemployed men to "stand in line almost every day in Chicago so that they can get a free cup of coffee and a piece of bread . . . and sleep on the floor in loghouses if they can obtain a bed for 5 or 10 cents."[38]

Skandinaven, defending a tailors' strike in Chicago in December, 1910, declared that social Darwinism indicated only one thing for the have-nots in America — misery. "When the strikers march through the streets, the people at large get glimpses of the privations these men and women suffer." Further, those who swallow the creed of the survival of the fittest forget "the wan, hopeless faces of underfed mothers, the frail bodies of overworked girls and the sinister gleams in the eyes of desperate men that must needs appeal to all who feel for their fellow men." Finally, "the most heartrending sights in this unfortunate struggle are not seen in public, but in the barren, desolate homes where children shiver from cold and cry for a crumb of bread."[39]

Throughout the period of Populism and Progressivism, the Norwegian editors were strongly prolabor. They were apostles of community spirit and social responsibility, and uncommonly egalitarian. These attitudes perhaps suggest why *Sioux Falls Posten* asked the

[37] *Syd Dakota Ekko*, March 6, 1902; *Skandinaven*, October 24, 1902.
[38] *Fram*, January 24, 1902; *Fergus Falls Ugeblad*, February 21, 1912.
[39] *Skandinaven*, December 16, 1910.

meat industrialist Jonathan Armour in 1909 to set "up a pension fund for his thousands of workers . . . who helped him and his firm to earn those millions of dollars." This view perhaps accounts for the lack of Norwegian-American John Deeres or Andrew Carnegies.[40]

Two of the most successful Norwegian-American businessmen in the late nineteenth century were Nelson Olson Nelson and John A. Johnson. Nelson forged the N. O. Nelson Company of St. Louis into one of America's largest building and supply corporations in the 1880's. Johnson built the Gisholt Machine Company of Madison, Wisconsin, into one of the leaders in the machine-tool industry by the 1890's. Yet neither was a "typical" American industrialist — neither was a social Darwinist. On the contrary, both introduced profit-sharing plans — Nelson in 1886, Johnson in 1895 — and both acknowledged the plight of the workingman in America. Indeed, as Agnes M. Larson explains in a recent biography, "Johnson's concern for the men who worked for him was not merely theoretical. In the days before pensions, unemployment insurance, and social security, his solicitude for their welfare continued beyond their last day's service in the shop or office." For example, to aid the elderly, Johnson "began planning to establish a home for veteran workmen when age made it impracticable for them to continue to be actively employed. For men who had no better place, there had been only the county poor farm. Feeling a strong personal responsibility for those who had helped him build his businesses, Johnson now had in mind a sort of haven of refuge where men advanced in age could live in comfort surrounded by kindness and good will. In his late sixties, Johnson was able to make all necessary arrangements for the center which he named the Gisholt Home for the Aged."[41]

Long before the era of pensions, Norwegian-American editors revealed a marked concern for the weaker and poorer members of society. Before the days of unemployment insurance and social security, they expressed communal values, fought for human rights, and responded favorably to the politics of reform.

[40] *Sioux Falls Posten* (Sioux Falls, S. D.), August 12, 1909.

[41] Agnes M. Larson, *John A. Johnson: An Uncommon American*, 188–190, 238 (Northfield, 1969). The words quoted are on page 238.

IV

The Politics of Reform

From the 1890's to World War I, Midwestern Norwegians thus were active leaders in the reform movement. Their role in the politics of protest in the Dakotas, Minnesota, and Wisconsin was, in fact, second to that of no other ethnic group. The degree of their protest also was second to none. Agrarian radicalism in the Norwegian-American community was affected by geography and economic conditions — from diversified agriculture in Wisconsin to one-crop farming in North Dakota, from high interest rates to low farm prices. But these factors hardly explain the consistency of Norwegian agrarian radicalism throughout the western Middle West. The common thread apparently was, as Jackson K. Putnam says, that these immigrants "brought with them a tradition of rural radicalism."[1]

In Norway they had resisted privilege and aristocracy and had favored a more equitable distribution of wealth. They had proclaimed communal values and scorned the principles of self-help and unregulated capitalism. As Robert Wilkins suggests, "they were

[1] Jackson K. Putnam, "The Socialist Party of North Dakota, 1902–1918," 27, unpublished master's thesis, University of North Dakota, 1956.

predominantly supporters of the . . . left in Norway, who from their Minnesota and Dakota homes sent moral and financial assistance to the left-wing leaders . . . for the fight against entrenched privilege in the homeland."[2]

In America these Norwegians flocked to the political left. From Ignatius Donnelly's time to that of Floyd B. Olson, their record of backing radical leaders and programs was phenomenal. Some joined the Socialist party. Many preferred the left wing of the Republican party. A multitude enlisted in the Populist coalition, the Nonpartisan League, and the Farmer-Labor party. Wilkins claims that in North Dakota thousands "of Norwegian farmers . . . who had been peasants in Norway were ardent socialists." They adopted the Nonpartisan League of A. C. Townley, which, as the *Grand Forks Herald* said, made the state "the socialistic laboratory of the country." They espoused the left-wing Republicanism of Peter Norbeck, which Gilbert Fite contends "led the South Dakota farmers a considerable distance along the road of state socialism." In Wisconsin they championed the social democracy of Robert M. La Follette, who, in the opinion of Robert Maxwell, systematically introduced the concept of government intervention to solve state problems. In Minnesota, they voted for the Farmer-Labor party of Floyd B. Olson, and, according to George H. Mayer, wrote one of the most radical programs "ever drawn up by an American party actually holding political power."[3]

In the late nineteenth century, thousands of Norwegians in the Dakotas and Minnesota quit the Republican party for the Farmers' Alliance and the Populist party. In North Dakota one Norwegian politician explained the anger of his countrymen: "The fact is this, that there is little or no faith in either of the great political parties. People out here are sighing under heavy oppressions from monopolists and high taxes to eastern manufacturers." Hence, "they have no confidence in the promises of the G.O.P. as most of their oppressors

[2] Robert P. Wilkins, "North Dakota and the European War, 1914–1917," 10, unpublished doctoral dissertation, University of West Virginia, 1954; Larsen, *A History of Norway*, 433–436, 454.

[3] Wilkins, "North Dakota and the European War," 11; Robinson, *History of North Dakota*, 288, 343; Gilbert C. Fite, *Peter Norbeck: Prairie Statesman*, 93 (Columbia, Mo., 1948); Maxwell, *La Follette*, 59–61; George H. Mayer, *The Political Career of Floyd B. Olson*, 170–172 (Minneapolis, 1951).

belong to it." At a meeting of irate Norwegian Republicans in Fargo, the following resolution was passed: "That we approve of the platform of the Farmers' Alliance and pledge our hearty sympathy and active cooperation and moral support to its policy."[4]

This story was repeated in Minnesota. Indeed, *Heimdal*, a Norwegian-language paper in St. Paul, insisted that "more than half of the Alliance in this state are Norwegians." George M. Stephenson, in his biography of John Lind, agreed. The Norwegians especially, he said, "were showing signs of dissatisfaction with the party that had held undisputed sway in the state since the election of Governor Ramsey. Political observers reported that the Norwegians were going into the Farmers' Alliance, whereas the Swedes remained loyal to their old allegiance." Underscoring this shift, thousands of Norwegians voted in 1890 for Sidney M. Owen, the first gubernatorial candidate of the Minnesota Farmers' Alliance. Although Owen lost to the Republican nominee, William R. Merriam, it was not for want of support from the Norwegian farmers. As J. J. Skordalsvold put it: "At the election 25,000 Norwegian-born farmers turned their backs upon Mr. Merriam and voted for Mr. Owen for governor."[5]

John M. Hetland of Halstad, Minnesota, deserted Merriam in 1890. In a letter to the editor of the *Norman County Herald*, he explained why: "The Republican party started with good principles and the farmers followed." But the Republicans "have ruined us as a class of people, and by putting party before men they have been able to elect millionaires and railroad agents." In April, 1890, N. L. Nelson of Ada leveled precisely the same charge at the two major parties. In both cases the leaders, he said, "are millionaires, own railroads and protected factories, and have the same interests to defend." They were like Tweedledum and Tweedledee. Thus, "When you hear these fellows quarreling about the tariff and other things you would almost think they were ready to pull each other's hair. But this is all for effect. They are merely throwing bones to us poor innocents to fight over while they are getting away with the meat."[6]

[4] *The North*, July 10, August 7, 1889.
[5] Editorial from *Heimdal* (St. Paul), quoted in *The North*, June 8, 1892; George M. Stephenson, *John Lind of Minnesota*, 119 (Minneapolis, 1935); *The North*, August 10, 1892.
[6] *Norman County Herald* (Ada, Minn.), April 11, May 2, 1890.

For the Norwegians, reform and radical third parties were indispensable. "It is encouraging to note," Tollef Benson of Ada commented, "how thinking men in our own locality constantly desert the old parties and join the reformers, while no one goes the other way." J. L. Mjolsness, inviting others to heed his example, said: "Crack the nutshell young man and see that a reform club is for the improvement of all who want to join." Others were far more indignant. As N. L. Nelson remarked, "I have talked to democrats and republicans and find that there is a secret yearning for a revolution." Speaking for a host of Norwegian farmers in the Red River Valley, J. G. Wangberg declared: "Faith in the republican and democratic party is fading away with the prosperity of the people and it is only a question of time until the parties must go or else the people. Which do you prefer? I prefer to have the people stay and I stay with the people as I'm turning socialist."[7]

The estimate that 25,000 Minnesota farmers abandoned the Republican party in 1890 is reaffirmed by the voting pattern for governor in Otter Tail and Polk counties in 1888 and 1890. There the Norwegians were thickly settled, and the Alliance was powerful. Scandinavians comprised 25 per cent of the population of Otter Tail County by 1890. In some townships the percentage was even higher. In Folden Township they numbered 262 of the 508 residents by 1895 — in Norwegian Grove Township, 306 of the 739. By 1890 Scandinavians were 30 per cent of the population in Polk County. They comprised 40 per cent of the population in Badger, Brislet, Eden, Lessor, Higdem, River Falls, and Winger townships by 1895.[8]

In 1888 there was no Alliance candidate for governor of Minnesota, but one appeared in 1890. There were only two major nominees for governor in 1888 — William R. Merriam for the Republicans, Thomas Wilson for the Democrats. In 1890, by contrast, there were three major candidates — Merriam, Wilson, and Owen. In Otter Tail County Merriam captured 3,368 votes to 2,170 for Wilson in 1888. But in 1890, Merriam slipped to 1,495, Wilson to 1,042, and Owen, the Alliance candidate, triumphed with 3,179. Merriam easily carried

[7] *Norman County Herald*, March 16, May 18, June 15, 1894.
[8] Michael L. Olson, "Scandinavian Immigrant Farmer Participation in Agrarian Unrest in Western Minnesota," 38–41, unpublished honors thesis, St. Olaf College, 1965.

Norwegian Grove Township in 1888. In 1890 there were 2 votes for
Merriam, 1 for Wilson, 87 for Owen. Merriam thrashed his opposition in Polk County in 1888, but two years later Owen swept the
county with 4,284 votes. In townships like Higdem, the vote was
even more lopsided — Merriam pocketed 3 votes, Wilson 2, Owen 86.
In Badger and Eden townships, Owen garnered every vote.[9]

Although Merriam was re-elected in 1890, the Norwegian protest
vote for Owen had an enormous impact on the Minnesota Republican party, and compelled it to acknowledge the burgeoning radicalism and political clout of the Norwegian Americans. It forced the
party to consider the nomination of a Norwegian for governor in
1892. As John D. Hicks records, the Republicans "proposed to 'pull the
whole Alliance back into the Republican party' by the nomination
for governor of Knute Nelson, whose stand on public questions . . .
had been so far in harmony with Alliance views that in 1890 the
revolting farmers could scarcely be restrained from adopting him
into their fold and nominating him for governor. . . . Nelson, moreover, was a leader among the Scandinavians, and . . . was 'supposed to carry the Norwegian vote of the State in the coat-tail
pocket of his trousers.' If anyone could win for the Republicans,
certainly Nelson was the man."[10]

But the response of the Norwegian agrarian leftists to the Knute
Nelson candidacy was generally negative. H. G. Stordock of Rothsay, for example, complained that Nelson had surrendered to the
native Americans. Writing him in March, 1892, Stordock said: "The
silk stocking element in the Republican party has always opposed
you until now. I do not think that they love you now but it is
because it is not certain about their chestnuts unless some one 'pulls
them out of the fire' for them and they have selected you for that
as being the proper party." Further, "The most bitter opposition
you will meet will be from Norwegians. . . . If the Alliance stays
together and re-nominates Owen he would get four fifths of the votes
around here." The socialist editor of *Dakota* in Fargo, Lauritz L.
Stavnheim, muttered that Nelson had betrayed the reform move-

[9] Olson, "Scandinavian Immigrant Farmer Participation," 52–54.
[10] John D. Hicks, "The People's Party in Minnesota," in *Minnesota History*,
8:544 (November, 1924).

ment. "The Scandinavians have lost their faith in Knute Nelson. There is no use trying to conceal this truth, and the sooner both he and his friends acknowledge this, the better." *Folkets Advokat*, a Norwegian-Swedish paper in Minneapolis, lamented that Nelson had capitulated to the plutocrats. Hence, "We hope our countrymen in Minnesota are too patriotic to risk the welfare of the state by voting for a monopolists' candidate because he happened to be born in one of the Scandinavian countries." [11]

Meanwhile, other ethnic groups, from Swedes to native Americans, were disturbed by Nelson's nomination for quite dissimilar reasons. They alleged that the Norwegians were systematically taking over the Minnesota Republican party. They protested that the Norwegians were altogether too combative in the cockpit of politics. *Svenska Kuriren* (Chicago), a Swedish paper, chided the Norwegians. In an editorial of August, 1892, it said that the Republican party in Minnesota "has nominated its candidates. Among these are:

For Governor	A Norwegian
For Secretary of State	A Norwegian
For Auditor	A Norwegian

The Swedes have simply been duped once more. The Scandinavian comedy has been acted as successfully as usual, the Norwegians speaking in the name of the Scandinavians. Why should not the Swedes of Minnesota for once think of themselves without forever allowing themselves to be led like cattle to the Republican ballot box?" A Swedish-American newspaper in St. Paul, *Minnesota Posten*, agreed, but it hinted that possibly the Swedes should imitate the Norwegians. Indeed, "one thing is certain, they have given our countrymen an illustrious example. . . . On the authority of the Norwegians themselves Mr. Owen received 25,000 Norwegian farmers' votes in 1890." Hence, "In 1892 Ignatius Donnelly ought to get at least as many Swedish votes." *Facklan*, a Swedish newspaper in Kansas City, Missouri, adopted the same thesis: "Our brothers the Norwegians are distinguishing themselves. . . . Now and then we

[11] H. G. Stordock to Knute Nelson, March 19, 1892, Knute Nelson Papers, Minnesota Historical Society; *Dakota* and *Folkets Advokat* are quoted in *The North*, February 24, August 24, 1892.

actually wish that we Swedes, too, had a little of that Norwegian dauntlessness."[12]

But *Svenska Kuriren* was not the only Swedish-American paper to needle the Norwegians for their political pugnacity. Sufficient disparagement appeared in the press to oblige the editor of *The North* to defend his countrymen. "On the whole," he wrote, "the history of Minnesota state politics will not uphold the assertion about the Norwegians having antagonized the Swedes. To be sure, citizens of the former nationality have held more offices than the latter, but this is due to conditions in which the alleged Norwegian selfishness cuts no figure at all. Among these must be counted the fact that the political unrest peculiar to the last few years has taken a firm hold upon the Norwegians of the state, while as yet the 'Swedes' hardly have been touched by it. This again has resulted in the election to office of more of the former class."[13]

Knute Nelson's nomination in 1892 ruffled the native Americans too; many, in fact, were indignant. The editor of the *Rush City Post* declared that Nelson "and all others similarly situated would stand immeasurably higher in the estimation of his fellow citizens by declining such honors for this reason: I AM NOT A NATIVE-BORN AMERICAN CITIZEN." The *St. Paul Dispatch* was equally positive: "As Mr. Nelson is to secure the Republican nomination because he is a Norwegian, let us inquire whether . . . in fact as well as logically it does not involve the establishment of a Scandinavian state government in this state." F. W. Seeley, an aide to a former Republican governor of Minnesota, amplified this argument in August, 1892. "I never expected to be called upon," he said, "to criticize the course of our party managers in this state on the nationality question." But, "In looking over the present and prospective personnel of the state officers, I find a Scandinavian governor, a Scandinavian secretary of state, a Scandinavian state auditor, [and] a Scandinavian clerk of the supreme court." And, "I find native Americans holding but two elective offices. . . . Here we have, or probably

---

[12] These newspapers are quoted in *The North*, June 29, August 10, 17, 31, 1892.
[13] *The North*, October 12, 1892.

will have after January 1 next, a state government administered almost wholly by foreign-born citizens."[14]

The *St. Paul Pioneer Press*, on the other hand, defended the strategy of the state Republican party in 1892 — if only because Nelson's "nomination would gratify that large Scandinavian element of the Republican party to which it owes so many of its triumphs in the past, and would bring back to its standard thousands who have been enticed into the ranks of the Alliance." In part, that happened. Without Knute Nelson heading up the state Republican ticket in 1890, Sidney M. Owen and the Farmers' Alliance bagged twenty-four counties in the contest for governor. With Knute Nelson, two years later, the Republican party held Ignatius Donnelly and the Populist party to merely six counties in the election. Nevertheless, the *St. Paul Pioneer Press* underrated the extent of radicalism in the Norwegian-American community. The Norwegians did not switch, even for one of their countrymen.[15]

H. G. Stordock of Rothsay warned Nelson in March, 1892, that the "most bitter opposition you will meet will be from Norwegians." John M. Hetland of Halstad and N. L. Nelson of Ada voiced the same argument. From *Folkets Advokat* in Minneapolis to *Red River Dalen* in Crookston, the radical Norwegian press discredited Nelson. The Norwegian Populists of Clay County passed a resolution declaring that Nelson's nomination was hardly "sufficient bait to cause a single Scandinavian adherent of the People's party to abandon its principles." The major principle was stated by *Red River Dalen*: "Nationalization ought to be the chief aim of the convention at Omaha. This ought to be a characteristic of the People's party. Nationalization not only of the liquor traffic, but also of the railroad and express traffic, of the telegraph and telephone service, of mines and oil wells etc."[16]

Stordock's prognostication was confirmed in Polk and Otter Tail counties. In the balloting for governor in 1892, Ignatius Donnelly whipped Nelson in Polk County, 3,183 to 1,267. In seven markedly

[14] *The North*, August 10, 24, 1892; *St. Paul Dispatch*, July 11, 1892.
[15] *St. Paul Pioneer Press*, July 1, 1892; Olson, "Scandinavian Immigrant Farmer Participation," 52–54.
[16] Dora J. Gunderson, "The Settlement of Clay County, Minnesota, 1870–1900," 75–77, unpublished master's thesis, University of Minnesota, 1929; *Red River Dalen*, quoted in *The North*, May 18, 1892.

Scandinavian townships, Donnelly's margin over Nelson was even more decisive — 52 to 14 in Badger, 13 to 6 in Brislet, 42 to 2 in Eden, 43 to 15 in Higdem, 89 to 12 in Lessor, 35 to 7 in River Falls, and 118 to 4 in Winger. In Otter Tail County, Nelson squeezed out a victory, 2,025 to 1,844. But in Folden and Norwegian Grove townships, where the Scandinavians comprised half of the population, Nelson fared badly. Donnelly won 87 to 4 in Folden, 65 to 22 in Norwegian Grove.[17]

Rural Norwegians were hardly alone in subscribing to the politics of agrarian radicalism in the 1890's. Michael Barone, in a paper on the politics of Minneapolis and St. Paul in the period from 1890 to 1905, maintains that a large number of urban Norwegians also championed the politics of protest. Many in the Twin Cities quit the Republican party for the Farmers' Alliance in 1890. In fact, as Barone observes about Minneapolis, "The wards where the Republican percentage dropped the most . . . and where the Farmers' Alliance candidates gained the most votes were, with one exception, the most Scandinavian." In those wards, over 17 per cent of the residents were born in Norway, Sweden, or Denmark. In St. Paul, he contends, the same pattern emerged: "The three wards with the largest percentages of Scandinavian-born persons . . . produced the greatest Republican losses in the city."[18]

The radicalism of the urban Scandinavians continued after 1890. Many in Minneapolis and St. Paul, for example, favored the Populist party. Throughout the 1890's in the Twin Cities, the Scandinavians "were the most volatile element." They were the most willing to embrace the politics of protest. Further, "it was primarily among Scandinavians that the Populists' appeals for working class support found any reward at all." Indeed, "Populism, despite its constant appeals for labor support, apparently received, not a labor vote, but a Scandinavian vote, in Minneapolis and St. Paul — the largest cities in which the Populists made a strong showing."[19]

Despite opposition from the radical Norwegians, Knute Nelson was elected governor of Minnesota in 1892. He was hardly a reac-

---

[17] Olson, "Scandinavian Immigrant Farmer Participation," 52–54; Minnesota, *Legislative Manual*, 1893, p. 424–426, 428–430.
[18] Michael Barone, "The Social Basis of Urban Politics: Minneapolis and St. Paul, 1890–1905," 1–5, unpublished honors thesis, Harvard University, 1965.
[19] Barone, "The Social Basis of Urban Politics," 8–23.

tionary, however; his Republicanism, in fact, was left of center. Like many Norwegians, Nelson supposed that his party remained the best hope for lasting reform in America. Lecturing a gathering of reform-minded farmers in October, 1890, he fused Progressivism and Republicanism: "The feeling of communism has sometimes been pretty strong within my breast." But "To my friends in the Farmer's alliance who feel with me that there are certain reforms to be accomplished, I have this to say: I know how you feel, but I am convinced that the best place in which to accomplish these reforms is in the ranks of the Republican party."[20]

For some time, Nelson had demanded the regulation of American corporate capitalism. He had pressed for a more equitable distribution of wealth and had questioned the ethos of unbridled individualism. In June, 1887, he put it this way: "Individuals have been aggrandized or crushed; special business interests have been fostered . . . and cities and villages have, with the exception of a few highly favored places and terminals, been ruthlessly smothered and reduced to a state of helplessness and apathy by these great corporations with an utter and complete obliviousness to all our intuitive and acquired notions of justice and equality." Finally, "The old order of things must pass away, and the new order of things based upon firmness and equality . . . must take its place."[21]

Nelson was a less zealous reformer as the gubernatorial candidate for the Republican party in 1892. But upon securing the governorship of Minnesota, he was prepared to utilize state power to solve problems. Arthur Naftalin maintains that during the Nelson administration "the Populists co-operated with the Republicans and achieved satisfaction on a number of issues." The legislature, for example, provided for state inspection of all country elevators. Minnesota farmers were empowered to erect independent elevators on the railroad right of way, and the railroad corporations were obliged to furnish sidetrack facilities. A law was even enacted authorizing the erection of a state-owned elevator, but the Minnesota Supreme Court declared it unconstitutional. For labor, a law was ratified fixing safeguards for dangerous industrial machinery and placing

[20] *Martin County Sentinel* (Fairmont, Minn.), October 24, 1890.
[21] *Daily Pioneer Press* (St. Paul and Minneapolis), June 8, 1887, quoted from a clipping in the Nelson Papers.

large state corporations under surveillance of the state bureau of labor.[22]

Another Norwegian who served as governor in the 1890's was Andrew E. Lee. A Populist, he was elected to office in South Dakota in 1896. Lee, a radical, repeatedly censured the "robber barons" and advocated the strict regulation of their corporations. But he warned: "If their absolute control cannot be accomplished by legislation, in my opinion the only remedy remaining is government ownership of transportation and other vast industries that are now being manipulated by the capitalists directly against the interests of the masses."[23]

During Lee's governorship, to 1900, some notable reforms were adopted by the South Dakota legislature. Approval of the Palmer-Wheeler Act was one break-through that enabled the railroad commission to superintend all lines in the state and to set maximum rate schedules. It authorized the state board of equalization to appraise railway property. Another law was enacted to block "large cattle companies from evading taxes in unorganized counties." Finally, the legislature backed a constitutional amendment sanctioning the initiative and referendum. The voters of South Dakota sustained the amendment in the general election of 1898.[24]

The Norwegian Americans played a principal role in the politics of Minnesota and the Dakotas during the 1890's. But after 1900 their participation in the protest movement was even more emphatic — especially in Wisconsin and North and South Dakota. In all three states, political reform groups captured power during the Progressive period, and the Norwegians were key leaders. They endorsed sweeping programs ranging from liberal to radical and supplied a goodly portion of the momentum for Middle Western Progressivism.

In Wisconsin, the Norwegians welcomed the election of Robert M. La Follette to the governorship in 1900 as the prelude to a new reform era. They cheered his struggle to fashion a social democracy. They also supported his efforts to regulate the railroads and public

[22] Arthur Naftalin, "The Tradition of Protest and the Roots of the Farmer-Labor Party," in *Minnesota History*, 35:61 (June, 1956); Hicks, in *Minnesota History*, 8:546; Martin W. Odland, *The Life of Knute Nelson*, 180–183 (Minneapolis, 1926).

[23] Lee to Joseph D. Sayers, July 6, 1899, Lee Papers.

[24] Herbert Schell, *History of South Dakota*, 236–238 (Lincoln, Neb., 1961); Charles J. Dalthorp, ed., *South Dakota's Governors*, 9 (Sioux Falls, S.D., 1953).

utilities, to enact laws governing workmen's compensation and controlling employers, to reorganize the system of taxation, and to establish an industrial commission. But, as *Skandinaven* suggested in 1906: "The Norwegians did not march into the La Follette camp; he came into their camp." Thus they had "fought with La Follette, not because he . . . presented a single principle of reform that was new to them, but because they found him to be a fearless foe of public abuses, an able champion of things that should be done, a fighter of skill and courage, a man to lead a fight in the field and win it."[25]

Not all Norwegians in Wisconsin lauded La Follette's programs. Rasmus B. Anderson, a onetime iconoclast, disliked him: "I have not been at all in sympathy with the political principles and measures that he has advocated." Rather, "I have no faith in his so-called 'reforms.'" But Anderson was a political anomaly in the Norwegian community; he himself said: "Politically I was friendless among the Norwegians because I was a stalwart Republican while they were nearly all enthusiastic admirers and supporters of La Follette." Further, Anderson admitted, "the reformer succeeded in getting a strong hold on the Norwegian group of citizens in Wisconsin. In every Norwegian community in the state there was the greatest enthusiasm for 'Bob' La Follette."[26]

In *La Follette and the Rise of the Progressives in Wisconsin*, Robert Maxwell writes that La Follette "had lived in a Norwegian neighborhood as a boy and spoke the language to some extent." Hence, "'Our Bob' was a great favorite among them, and he spared no effort to retain their friendship and affection." In election after election, the Wisconsin Norwegians contributed practically a bloc vote for the Progressives. "Even the staunchest stalwarts conceded that they offered 'quite a barren soil on which to sow anti-La Follette seed.' The careful tending of this potential election crop was one of the important functions of La Follette's new progressive machine." Compared to the Germans, moreover, the Norwegians were veritable radicals. In fact, "The Germans of Wisconsin, the state's largest ethnic group, were largely individualistic in politics.

[25] *Skandinaven*, August 1, 1906.
[26] Anderson, *Life Story*, 574–649. The words quoted are from pages 608, 616, 626, 649.

Although staunch supporters of representative government, they were generally conservative and lacked the political solidarity that characterized the Norwegians."[27]

A score of Norwegians occupied important political offices in Wisconsin during the Progressive years. James O. Davidson, a native of Norway, assumed the governorship in 1906 after La Follette stepped up to the United States Senate. Long a partisan of La Follette, Davidson had been his lieutenant governor from 1903 to 1906. Nils P. Haugen was the pre-eminent figure on the tax commission from 1901 to 1921. Herman Ekern, speaker of the Wisconsin assembly from 1907 to 1911, was chosen insurance commissioner in 1911. Three Norwegians filled the office of state treasurer during the period, and two gained seats in the United States Congress.[28]

The political gambit of the reformers in Wisconsin was simple — advance the politics of protest through the Republican party. To the extent that this took place during La Follette's era, Norwegians provided much of the thrust. During Davidson's two terms as governor, some significant reform measures were passed. The Public Utilities Act of 1907 placed the gas, water, electric light, and telephone companies under the control of the railroad commission. In the same session, far-reaching reforms regulating insurance companies were approved. Before Davidson vacated the governorship, a graduated income tax designed to supplant the inequitable personal property tax was adopted by the Wisconsin assembly in 1911.[29]

Nils P. Haugen, the first Republican antimachine candidate to campaign for governor, was named by Governor La Follette to the tax commission in 1901. This body, dominated by Haugen, was central "to the whole success of the progressive reform program in Wisconsin." It conceived many of the key La Follette tax reforms, such as the ad valorem railroad tax, the inheritance tax, and the graduated income tax. The commission was a major instrument in shaping social democracy in Wisconsin. By World War I, Wisconsin was the precursor in a nationwide reform movement. As Robert

[27] Maxwell, La Follette, 59–61.
[28] Maxwell, La Follette, 59–61; Norlie, Norwegian People in America, 489–492.
[29] Maxwell, La Follette, 96–127.

Maxwell suggests, "Wisconsin perhaps offered the most striking example of the reforms and innovations that characterized progressivism. Although neither the first nor the most radical state in its proposals, Wisconsin inaugurated, under the leadership of Robert M. La Follette, Sr. and others, a comprehensive program of political, economic, and social reforms that affected the life of every person in the state. These reforms, in turn, served as models that were copied, in whole or in part, by many other states and by the national government."[30]

The Norwegians were also in the vanguard of the protest movement in North Dakota. They were far more radical there than elsewhere and far more numerous. Thus, their political leverage and sentiments were expressed more bluntly. A basically one-crop agriculture in North Dakota aggravated the plight of the farmers. Hence, their radical convictions surfaced more readily.

Elwyn B. Robinson maintains that the "Norwegian immigrants . . . brought radicalism to North Dakota." They injected it into several parties and movements during the Progressive era — the Socialist party, the Republican party, the Equity movement, the Nonpartisan League. A number of Norwegians, for example, were attracted to the North Dakota Socialist party, which began its activity in 1900, when Arthur Basset organized the first socialist club in Fargo. Two years later, the Socialist party in North Dakota was organized. Its leaders accented rural problems — from capitalist exploitation of the farmer and high interest rates to insufficient farm income and increasing mortgage foreclosures. Meanwhile, as Jackson K. Putnam asserts, many Norwegians "found reason to retain their socialism in their new homeland. The North Dakota socialist leaders quickly capitalized on the Norwegian political heritage, and allowed them to form 'language locals' in affiliation with the state socialist party. These soon became popular and respectable organizations, the members considering themselves an intellectual elite in comparison with their American comrades whose socialist education was notoriously shallow."[31]

Robert L. Morlan says that the Socialist party "was more strongly

---

[30] Maxwell, *La Follette*, 5, 87–104.
[31] Robinson, *History of North Dakota*, 328–330; Putnam, "The Socialist Party," 27.

organized in North Dakota at this time than in any other agricultural state, having found fertile ground for complaint against the
existing order." By 1904, support for the party was shifting from the
eastern to the northwestern counties, where conditions were more
depressed. Arthur Le Sueur, a commanding figure among the socialists, moved to northwestern North Dakota, and, as Putnam explains,
"those contagious carriers of socialism, the Norwegians, were beginning to take up homesteads in this area, and, confronted with the
more severe agricultural difficulties there, they no doubt lost none
of their radical convictions." By 1912 there were 175 socialist clubs
in the state, and the top offices in Hillsboro, Rugby, and Minot were
controlled by socialists.[32]

Other Norwegians, including many radicals, were inclined to
back a variety of left-of-center Republican measures during the
Progressive period. For years, they sought to reform their party and
to subvert Alexander McKenzie's domination of it. As Robinson explains, the reformers "found their strongest support in the eastern
portion of the state, the region settled by Norwegians; McKenzie's
stronghold was the Missouri Slope and the area of heavy German
Russian settlement." To rid the party of McKenzie's machine, many
Norwegians were eager to retool the Scandinavian Republican
League. Their intentions had been spelled out several years earlier
by *Afholds-Basunen* of Hillsboro: "The Scandinavians of North
Dakota do not desire to fight a campaign on nationality lines." But
"if we are forced into such a fight by having the ablest and most
honest men in the state crowded aside because they have Scandinavian blood in their veins — then we will fight to the end and deal
painful blows. . . . Why should we, the countrymen of Leif Erickson, yield the ground to other nationalities in Leif Erickson's own
country?"[33]

A. A. Trovaten, one of the owners of *Fram*, was president of the
Scandinavian Republican League. P. O. Thorson, the business manager of *Normanden*, was its secretary. John Sorley, a Grand Forks
lawyer and long-time member of the legislature, was one of the

---

[32] Robert L. Morlan, *Political Prairie Fire*, 23 (Minneapolis, 1955); Putnam,
"The Socialist Party," 23–31.
[33] Robinson, *History of North Dakota*, 256; Andrew A. Bruce, *Non-Partisan
League*, 29–32 (New York, 1921); *Afholds-Basunen*, quoted in *The North*,
March 23, 1892.

league's most combative members. Andrew A. Bruce comments that Sorley and his friends expedited the formation of the Nonpartisan League by "organizing [their] countrymen and formulating their protest against the dominant Scotch McKenzie-McCumber-Hansbrough autocracy." Sorley coupled this protest against the Yankee Republicans with one of his favorite themes, exploitation, and he informed the Norwegian farmer in North Dakota "that the independence which he had fought for in Norway . . . was being denied to him in North Dakota. He [*the farmer*] was told that in the place of the hated aristocracy of blood and of the old world there was a new aristocracy of money and corporate power." [34]

For precisely the same reason — exploitation and the protest against it — the equity movement lured a host of Norwegian farmers. Organized in 1902, the American Society of Equity was one of the first farm orders to win some degree of prominence in the twentieth century. The purpose of the equity movement was simple — to keep farm products off the market until fixed prices were secured. The American Society of Equity, according to Theodore Saloutos, "attracted its first substantial support in the wheat-growing river counties of the upper Mississippi Valley. . . . Here the Scandinavian element was strong, and blood ties tended to supplement the economic unity which stemmed from the common problems experienced by grain growers." Further, "The marketing program of Equity was aided, no doubt, by the presence of large numbers of Scandinavians in the spring wheat area. . . . There is reason to believe that during the Equity period more cooperative stores, creameries, and elevators existed among the Scandinavians of the Northwest than among the native-Americans." [35]

The major goal of the Equity Society was to control the wheat crop. North Dakota provided the greatest support for the holding action. Theodore G. Nelson and a troupe of trained organizers, sustained by the large percentage of Norwegians, signed up ten thousand farmers in 1907. But by 1908, some members of Equity, de-

[34] Løvoll, in *Norwegian-American Studies*, 24:88; Bruce, *Non-Partisan League*, 29–32.

[35] Theodore Saloutos and John D. Hicks, *Agricultural Discontent in the Middle West, 1900–1939*, 111–134 (Madison, Wis., 1951).

ciding that holding actions were ineffectual, chose to concentrate on co-operative marketing. They established the Equity Cooperative Exchange. Meanwhile, a growing number of North Dakota farmers believed that one solution to the marketing problem would be the creation of state-owned terminal elevators. By 1915 the people of North Dakota had twice approved constitutional amendments providing for such elevators by three-to-one margins. While the legislature debated the merits of a terminal elevator bill in 1915, the North Dakota Equity convention was meeting in Bismarck. Under the fiery leadership of George S. Loftus, the delegates endorsed the bill and trudged to the capitol to submit their demands. They were rebuffed and the bill was defeated. "The Equity convention," Robinson says, "quickly became a protest meeting; angry farmers argued long and bitterly with legislators. During one such argument late at night, Treadwell Twichell, a house member, was reported to have told the farmers that the running of the state was none of their business and to have jocularly advised them to 'go home and slop the hogs.' Twichell denied ever having said it, but the phrase became a fighting slogan of the Nonpartisan League."[36]

The phrase also soon became a battle cry for A. C. Townley. A former flax farmer at Beach and an organizer for the North Dakota Socialist party until 1914, Townley was in Bismarck when the legislature squelched the elevator bill. He reckoned that the farmers were ripe for action and decided to forge a new farmers' organization — the Nonpartisan League. Townley's scheme was brilliant — to endorse the socialist program of state ownership, to exploit the rural hatred for industrial capitalists, and to keep the League within the Republican party. Using the organizing gimmicks that had worked so well for the North Dakota Socialist party — from paid organizers and Ford cars to postdated checks and individual solicitation — Townley and his associates recruited an incredible 26,000 members by 1916.[37]

Many farmers in the state had long espoused socialistic ideas,

[36] Morlan, *Political Prairie Fire*, 18–23; Robinson, *History of North Dakota*, 330.

[37] Robinson, *History of North Dakota*, 327–335; Morlan, *Political Prairie Fire*, 20–25.

but not the Socialist party. For them, Townley's radical program was tailor-made — advocating public ownership of terminal elevators and packing plants as well as a system of state hail insurance and rural-credit banks. And his party — the Republican — was a traditional one. Counting on timeworn political loyalties, Townley hoped, by entering his candidates in primary elections, to gain control of North Dakota's majority party. "The League," as Morlan explains, "was one of the most striking attempts to actually so use the primary. It proposed to . . . make [the Republicans] truly express the will of the majority of the voters, and retain the benefits of its status arising from tradition and voter habit as well."[38]

An array of Norwegian farmers in the state, including socialists, left-of-center Republicans, and members of Equity, embraced the Nonpartisan League. Nicolay A. Grevstad, a prominent journalist, said that they were "roped in by league organizers in droves." He explained that, except for *Normanden*, hardly a Norwegian newspaper in North Dakota resisted the League. In defying it, *Normanden* estranged many of its readers; indeed, hundreds of farmers protested by canceling their subscriptions. In short, as Odd Sverre Løvoll contends, the Nonpartisan League "appealed strongly to many Norwegians. A large number of them had leftist sympathies, and even more of them had few misgivings about pursuing a radical solution to the problems that faced them."[39]

Many of these Norwegians were already involved in North Dakota politics. By 1916, two were already in the United States Congress — Henry T. Helgesen in the House and Asle J. Grønna in the Senate. By 1916, the Norwegians already controlled approximately 25 per cent of the seats in both houses of the legislature. In the same year, when the first slate of candidates was framed by the Nonpartisan League, some prominent Norwegians were included — A. T. Kraabel for lieutenant governor, S. A. Olsness for commissioner of insurance, John N. Hagen for commissioner of agriculture and labor, M. P. Johnson and Sam Aandahl for railroad commissioners. Except for P. M. Casey, the League nominee for state treasurer, all the

[38] Robinson, *History of North Dakota*, 329–333; Morlan, *Political Prairie Fire*, 33.
[39] Grevstad to Preus, July 25, 1917, Grevstad Papers; Løvoll, in *Norwegian-American Studies*, 24:92.

candidates endorsed by the League in 1916 triumphed in both the
Republican primary and the general election.[40]

The proposals of the North Dakota Nonpartisan League in 1916
signified, in the words of Robinson, "a broad experiment in state
socialism." They included state ownership of terminal elevators,
flour mills, packing houses, and cold-storage plants; state inspection
of grain and grain dockage; state hail insurance on the acreage tax
basis; and rural credit banks operated at cost. Between 1917 and
1919, most of the proposals were passed by the state legislature.
During the 1917 session a number of important measures were
enacted: a state grain-grading law, a state-bank deposit guarantee
law, a nine-hour-day law for women, a law to reduce the rate of
assessment on farm machinery, and one forbidding distinctions between long- and short-haul railroad rates.[41]

But it was the 1919 session of the legislature that ushered in a
far-reaching program of socialism. An industrial commission was
established to pilot all state business enterprises. The Bank of North
Dakota was instituted to act as sole depository for all state and local
government funds and to supply low-cost rural credits. The North
Dakota Mill and Elevator Association was created to provide for
the processing and marketing of farm products and to establish a
system of flour mills, elevators, plants, factories, and warehouses.
The Home Building Association was devised to construct houses for
low- and middle-income groups. Laws providing for a graduated
income tax, a minimum wage for women, and an eight-hour working
day were also passed by the legislature. "The state is now the
socialistic laboratory of the country," the *Grand Forks Herald* said
in March, 1919, "and unless the people veto the administration
measures the experiment soon will begin. . . . The most interesting
experiment in the history of the country will be carried out in this
state during the next two years." Thus the Nonpartisan League
radicalized North Dakota politics. Further, it "laid much of the
foundation of modern midwestern liberalism. It helped develop some
of the most independently minded electorates in the country. It

[40] Morlan, *Political Prairie Fire*, 51–53; North Dakota, *Legislative Manual*,
1916, p. 578–599.
[41] Robinson, *History of North Dakota*, 338–343; Morlan, *Political Prairie
Fire*, 23–27.

built one of the first successful alliances between farmers and organized labor, and gave birth to Minnesota's Farmer-Labor party."[42]

The Norwegians were a vigorous political force in South Dakota too. There they were the second largest ethnic group, outnumbered only by the Germans. But, as in Wisconsin, they were far more dogged in the field of politics. In 1917 the South Dakota house of representatives, for example, included at least twenty-two Norwegians but only three Germans. "The Norwegians," as Herbert S. Schell remarks, "have been especially important in South Dakota's history, and have furnished many outstanding leaders." Between 1896 and 1917, they helped to elect from their group three governors, one lieutenant governor, two state treasurers, two state superintendents of education, one secretary of state, and one auditor. And possibly the most outstanding of their political leaders was a radical Republican governor, Peter Norbeck.[43]

Norbeck's radicalism apparently surfaced only after his election in 1916. Before that time, he had been a progressive Republican, compassionate toward the poor and dispossessed. In a word, he had battled for the farmer and protested capitalist exploitation. Gilbert Fite, in his biography of Norbeck, argues that his progressive views "did not stem so much from intellectual conviction as from instinct. . . . He was never identified with the moneyed interests in the state. . . . It was not selfishness . . . that motivated him to go along with the progressives. He had an inherent sympathy for the common people, especially the farmers, and if beneficial legislation could be passed he favored it."[44]

Campaigning as a progressive Republican, Norbeck was elected to the state senate in 1908. By 1911 he was South Dakota chairman of the National Republican Progressive League. In 1914 he was chosen lieutenant governor. By 1916 he was being primed for the governorship. In this contest, Norbeck had the unflagging support of several groups — the South Dakota Scandinavian Republican League, friends in the legislature (especially Norwegians), and

[42] Robinson, *History of North Dakota*, 340–345; Morlan, *Political Prairie Fire*, 229–238, 359–361.
[43] *United States Census*, 1910, *Population*, 695; South Dakota, *Legislative Manual*, 1917, p. 644–678; Herbert S. Schell, *History of South Dakota*, 380 (Lincoln, Neb., 1961); Norlie, *Norwegian People in America*, 489–492.
[44] Fite, *Peter Norbeck*, 9–49.

farmers (especially Norwegians). By this time, he had a liaison man in virtually every precinct. "It is significant," Fite says, "that his organization was based strictly on the farm vote. He made relatively little effort to carry the larger towns. By working through and with a large number of devoted personal followers, and throwing his success into the hands of the ordinary dirt farmer, he built and maintained an unbeatable machine. The distribution of loaves and fishes played no prominent part during the formative period of his organization."[45]

Norbeck scored two easy victories in the election of 1916 — the first over two opponents in the Republican primary, the second over the Democratic candidate in the November balloting. In his first address to the legislature Norbeck pressed for the ratification of a rural credits plan, a hail-insurance scheme, a workmen's compensation law, a state-owned coal mine, and a system of state-owned terminal grain elevators. Further, he urged the approval of a program for the development of water-power sites and the protection of wildlife resources. The 1917 legislative session responded affirmatively. The proposals for rural credits and workmen's compensation were sustained. The legislature also passed resolutions referring twelve constitutional amendments to the voters — including those for state hail insurance, a state-owned cement plant, a state-owned hydroelectric project, and a system of state-owned grain elevators, warehouses, flour mills, and packing houses.[46]

By the end of the session, Norbeck was challenged by a new force in state politics — the Nonpartisan League. Indeed, the South Dakota branch of the League claimed a membership of 20,000 farmers in the spring of 1917. To curb it and to prepare for the next election, Norbeck harped upon several themes — his record, his radicalism, his ethnic origin. Regarding the record, he said: "First, we supported every good suggestion that the farmers made. Second, we did not even oppose their going into new experiments of uncertain value." As for his radicalism, he was equally candid: "Where men attempt to extort an unreasonable profit, it is the business of the government to step in and regulate it and where the

[45] Fite, *Peter Norbeck*, 28–49.
[46] Schell, *History of South Dakota*, 261–266; Fite, *Peter Norbeck*, 50–58.

regulation can be best had by government ownership and operation, this plan should be adopted."[47]

In the 1918 election, Norbeck defeated the candidates of both the Nonpartisan League and the Democratic party. The reform impulse of his first administration carried over to the second. Under his direction, the 1919 session of the legislature approved state ownership of a coal mine and a cement plant, a state hail-insurance program, and a state bonding department. Not everyone in South Dakota crowed over these radical undertakings. The editor of the *Aberdeen Daily News* denounced the Norbeck administration: "In its efforts to out-Townley Townley, it caused to be adopted a platform so radical that the Townley program was the extreme of conservation in comparison." But the Norwegian-American farmers praised his efforts. They lauded Norbeck, as Fite asserts, because he "led the South Dakota farmers a considerable distance along the road of state socialism."[48]

Norwegians were also active in the United States Congress during the Progressive period. Between 1900 and 1917, those in Wisconsin, North Dakota, South Dakota, and Minnesota elected three senators and ten congressmen from their group. The high point was in 1917, with two Norwegians in the Senate and eight in the House of Representatives. Like their counterparts in state politics, the Norwegians in Congress functioned within the Republican party and were clearly left of center. These politicians, representing practically every area of dense Norwegian settlement in the Middle West, voted as a bloc for major reform measures: the Hepburn Act, the Pure Food and Drug Act, a joint resolution for the income tax, the Mann-Elkins Act, the Warehouse Act, the woman suffrage amendment, the Child Labor Act, and the Adamson Act. Similarly, they jointly opposed the Underwood Tariff and the Clayton Antitrust Act. Apparently they divided on only one measure — the Federal Reserve Act.[49]

---

[47] Schell, *History of South Dakota*, 266–270; Fite, *Peter Norbeck*, 60–65.

[48] Schell, *History of South Dakota*, 266–270; Fite, *Peter Norbeck*, 68–93.

[49] Norlie, *Norwegian People in America*, 489–492; *Congressional Record*, 40:7088, 9075, 9084, 44:4120, 4440, 45:7375, 50:1386, 4617, 51:14610, 16344, 52:1483, 53:2035, 7271, 12313, 13608, 13655, 60:2773. For a listing of how Norwegians in Congress voted on important reform bills during the Progressive movement, see the appendix to this volume. Because the Federal Trades Com-

Interpreting the protest politics in America and in Congress, Senator Asle J. Grønna of North Dakota declared: "The Insurgent movement is more than a mere revolt against present party leaders in Congress. It will have failed its purpose if its result is merely the disposition of others following the same tactics." Hence, "It is a revolt against the system and policies for which the present leaders stand; it is a revolt against special privilege and against the control of legislation by certain large interests."[50]

The Norwegians in Congress, like their counterparts in state politics, flayed the big-money interests, protested the maldistribution of wealth, and condemned capitalist exploitation of the farmers. Congressman Haldor Boen of Minnesota had said that farming in America amounted to only "unremitting toil from early morn till late at night, from childhood to the grave. And when near the end of a busy life the weary worker views his or her possessions it is generally found that the chief item in the assets is the knowledge of dreary years spent in the production of wealth that has been enjoyed by others." And, he added, "Sobriety, industry, honesty, a fertile soil and good climate availeth not."[51]

During the years of Populism and Progressivism, not one Norwegian-American member of Congress was a social Darwinist, nor did any voice the laissez-faire theory. Most discounted the success myth and preached the advancement of the public good. As Representative Gilbert Haugen of Iowa contended: "Every man's duty, no matter what his political affiliation . . . is to strive to benefit this country, protect the weak, relieve the distressed, uplift humanity." Even Senator Nelson of Minnesota claimed that America had granted too many benefits "to the powerful and the rich" but only a mere pittance to "the laboring man, the poor," and "the struggling masses." The day of socialism for the rich and private enterprise for the poor was over. As Asle Grønna of North Dakota put it, "The

mission Act (known in the House as the Covington bill) passed the House by a voice vote, positions taken by Norwegian members cannot be determined. The two Norwegians in the Senate voted against it, and several speeches in the House by Norwegians indicate similar opposition. See *Congressional Record*, 51:13319.

[50] William W. Phillips, "The Growth of a Progressive: Asle J. Gronna," 52, unpublished master's thesis, University of North Dakota, 1952.

[51] *Faribault Republican*, February 14, 1894.

main business of the Government should be the promotion of the welfare of the people."[52]

Senator Knute Nelson was the most conservative Norwegian in Congress in the period 1901–17, and his conservatism seemed to deepen with the years. As a state politician in the late 1880's and early 1890's, he was sympathetic to the goals of agrarian radicalism. As a United States Senator, he was a left-of-center to moderate Republican. The only Norwegian in the House or Senate to support President Woodrow Wilson's policy of involvement in World War I, he was increasingly critical of radicalism in America, especially in the Norwegian-American community. But he was never a reactionary nor an advocate of the laissez-faire theory. Instead, as Millard L. Gieske suggests, he "tended to accept the need for greater national regulation over the economic order, though out of personal bias he preferred to speak in terms of 'remedial' legislation." Nelson himself clamored for the rigid enforcement of the Sherman Antitrust Act: "I regard the antitrust law of 1890 as, next to the Constitution of the United States, the most important law on the statute books, and the one that the people of the country stand in most need of. It is the only protection they have against the formation, the aggressions, and the inroads of trusts, monopolies, and combinations in restraint of trade."[53]

In the first decade of the twentieth century, one combination — the railway trust — was feared above all others by Norwegians in Congress. They sensed that its policies were related to other abuses in American capitalism. If the railroads could be prevented from charging discriminatory rates, Pandora's box might be shut: Standard Oil and the gigantic meat-packing companies would no longer be able to dictate freight rates. Smaller companies could compete with larger rivals, and farmers would be able to send products to market more cheaply.

In debating the Hepburn bill of 1906, the Norwegians in the House and Senate cashiered the ideology of rugged individualism. The "power to fix rates of transportation," as Representative Halvor Steenorson of Minnesota insisted, "is one too great to rest uncon-

[52] *Congressional Record*, 40:2175, 45:4431, 4513.
[53] Millard L. Gieske, "The Politics of Knute Nelson, 1912–1920," 60, 116–160, unpublished doctor's thesis, University of Minnesota, 1965.

trolled in private hands." Congressman Gilbert Haugen of Iowa agreed that the Interstate Commerce Commission should have full power to approve railroad rates because "it takes annually a billion dollars net profit to satisfy [the railroad owners'] greed." In short, as Senator Knute Nelson decided, the railroads, because they provided a public service, should be "subject, in consequence, to public control." After the Hepburn bill was enacted, giving the Interstate Commerce Commission the authority to set reasonable maximum rates and to prescribe uniform methods of accounting, Representative Andrew Volstead of Minnesota reminded Congress that "we must not persuade ourselves that we have reached the limit of what should be done." In fact, he wondered "why interstate telegraph and telephone lines should not be regulated the same as railway lines?"[54]

The Mann-Elkins Act, empowering the Interstate Commerce Commission to suspend new rail rates and to control the telephone, telegraph, cable, and wireless companies, was passed in 1910. But the Norwegians in Congress remained disgruntled with the pace of reform. Even the usually moderate Nelson was inclined to predict that "the day will come, unless the proper restraints are maintained, when the American people will be in the fangs of the trusts and combinations just as the poor French people were in the hands of their nobility prior to the great French revolution." Hence, "If we are not wise . . . the day will come . . . when the American people will resort to a revolution as the people of France had to do, but it will be a peaceful revolution — not as violent and repulsive as the French, but as thorough and effective in its results."[55]

Nelson's speech mirrored an increasing concern for reform politics in the Middle Western Norwegian community. Gilbert Haugen of Iowa, John Nelson of Wisconsin, and Steenorson and Volstead of Minnesota, campaigning as insurgents, were all re-elected to the House of Representatives in 1910. In North Dakota, two Norwegians were elected to Congress — Asle Grønna to the Senate, Henry Helgesen to the House. Grønna's brand of insurgency was defined by La Follette: "Latterly the Grønna type of patriotism has become so prevalent that the political doctors have seen fit to take notice

[54] *Congressional Record*, 39:181, 187–196 (appendix), 40:3840. See also *Congressional Record*, 40:140 (appendix).
[55] *Congressional Record*, 45:4514.

of it and its manifestations. They have classified and labeled it Insurgency. Which, defined from its manifestations, means simply a disposition to give high regard to the public welfare and to the wishes and interests of the people in the conduct of public affairs." [56]

The insurgent fight against "standpattism" was escalating all over the Middle West. But it was in southern Minnesota, the most conservative part of the state, where the insurgents scored one of their major upsets in the 1910 Congressional elections. In the first district's Republican primary the powerful chairman of the House appropriations committee, James A. Tawney, was bounced by a young half-Norwegian, half-Swedish lawyer, Sydney Anderson. "Tawney was the most influential standpatter to be unseated in 1910," Roger E. Wyman says, "and progressives around the nation rejoiced at this devastating blow to the Cannon organization." Discrediting Tawney's record on the tariff, trusts, and conservation, Anderson campaigned as an insurgent. "Anderson's heaviest vote," Wyman explains, "was polled in counties with large Scandinavian populations. Scandinavians were prominent among Anderson's campaign workers, and Norwegian progressives from Wisconsin campaigned for him. Several Tawney supporters lamented the solidarity of Scandinavians behind one of their own in the election." Anderson, after an easy victory in the general election, joined seven other Norwegians in the House and Senate. [57]

Despite the Congressional elections, approval of the Canadian reciprocal trade agreement in 1911 signaled that the so-called standpatters were still powerful. The Norwegian Americans in Congress charged that the agreement would profit only the big businessmen — the railroad titans, the millers, the meat packers. "The whole burden of reciprocity," Knute Nelson lamented, "is cast on the farmer. His products are the quid pro quo for the entire scheme. There is no reciprocity in any of his products." Thus, "The scheme is to give the Canadian farmers our market to the end that our manufacturers can secure a part of the Canadian market for their products." Asle Grønna charged that the American farmers were regularly sacrificed

[56] Norlie, *Norwegian People in America*, 489–492; Phillips, "The Growth of a Progressive," 104.

[57] Roger E. Wyman, "Insurgency in Minnesota: The Defeat of James A. Tawney in 1910," in *Minnesota History*, 40:317–329 (Fall, 1967); Norlie, *Norwegian People in America*, 489–492.

to the interests of the industrial capitalists. "Farmers who are asked to share their markets with the Canadian farmers," he said, "will derive no benefit from this agreement. It opens no new markets to them, and it reduces the duties on practically nothing that they buy."[58]

Norwegians in the House and Senate were equally outraged by President Woodrow Wilson's advocacy of the Underwood tariff proposal in 1913. All eight opposed this first building block in Wilson's New Freedom. Summing up the rationale for their opposition to the Underwood bill, Senator Grønna declared: "It is the principle of the Canadian reciprocity measure over again — free trade in the products that the farmer sells and protection in what he has to buy. The farmer is expected to sell in competition with the world and to buy in a protected market."[59]

Here was another example of the might of the industrial capitalists, of exploitation by the producers, of socialism for the rich and private enterprise for the poor. To Halvor Steenorson, it was an old story — the Underwood tariff was only "for the benefit of the manufacturing and commercial classes." To Gilbert Haugen of Iowa, it was "drawn so as to greatly reduce the duty or to put on the free list practically everything produced on the farms in the Northwest under the designation of raw materials, while the . . . manufactured articles . . . are protected by a high duty."[60]

Norwegian congressmen endorsed a reform amendment to the Federal Reserve bill that would have prohibited an officer or director of any national or state bank or trust company admitted to membership in a Federal Reserve bank from becoming an officer or director of any other bank or financial corporation. But five of the eight Norwegians in Congress voted against the final passage of the bill. "Instead of having a system of regional or reserve banks," Knute Nelson maintained, "we ought to have a large central bank, of nonvoting stock, subscribed by the people, under the absolute control of the Federal Government. Such a bank would be a great reservoir from which all national banks as well as state banks could at all times secure help in times of stress and emergency." Grønna, labeled with

[58] *Congressional Record,* 46:3664, 47:2082.
[59] *Congressional Record,* 50:1386, 4617, 51:16508.
[60] *Congressional Record,* 50:361 (appendix), 716.

La Follette of Wisconsin and George Norris of Nebraska as one of "the most hard-headed irreconcilables" in the Senate, reasoned that the bill would "legalize money trusts and credit trusts in the different sections of the country — not more than 12 nor less than 8." Further, "I do not believe it the part of wisdom to provide for the enormous aggregation of power in the different districts and leave this power in private control." Hence, control of the regional banks "should be in the hands of the Government." [61]

Not one Norwegian in the House or Senate voted for the Clayton antitrust bill. Their general reaction was a definite one — the bill would only enfeeble the Sherman Antitrust Act. Indeed, Grønna maintained that it was "toothless." Andrew Volstead of Minnesota responded similarly. He stressed that, under the Sherman Antitrust Act of 1890, the government had to prove only that a trust possessed the power to restrain trade. But under the Clayton plan, it had to demonstrate that a trust actually lessened competition. He warned, too, that a section in the bill permitted companies to invest in the stock of other corporations. In short, Volstead concluded that the "Clayton Antitrust Act is a distinct effort on the part of the administration to take the teeth out of the Sherman Act." [62]

The Norwegians in Congress, like their counterparts in state politics, consistently attacked the system of industrial capitalism. It exploited the genuine producers, led to an incredible maldistribution of wealth, and impoverished many. The Norwegians had come from a society where co-operation and a sense of community were stressed, where caring for the public good was axiomatic, where one of the most advanced welfare states in the world was being fashioned. From the beginnings of the Populist movement to the onset of World War I, they ranked second to no other Middle Western ethnic group in the role that they played in reform politics. But it was during the war that they achieved some of their greatest successes at the state level, that they participated in implementing a far-reaching program of socialism in North and South Dakota, and when, in and out of Congress, they raised their voices against President Wilson's policy of foreign involvement.

[61] *Congressional Record*, 50:5128, 51:456, 1039, 1230, 1464; Phillips, "The Growth of a Progressive," 124–132.
[62] *Congressional Record*, 51:9077–9081, 14610, 16344, 54:4952; Phillips, "The Growth of a Progressive," 133.

V

From War to Depression

From the beginning, Norwegian Americans in the Middle West resisted the entry of this country into World War I. Long opponents of corporate capitalism, they soon decided that industrialists and Wall Street speculators, in conjunction with English capitalists, were pushing America into war. As J. E. Engstad of Minneapolis declared: "It is the great money trust in the world that makes war."[1]

To Congressman John Nelson of Wisconsin the reason that many industrialists favored intervention was obvious: "Is it not human nature that . . . bankers who have loaned billions to one side, or manufacturers of war material who have sold billions of dollars' worth of munitions to one side, desire to see that side win with whom they have cast their lot?" Senator Asle Grønna of North Dakota charged that Wall Street speculators and bankers favored war: "I also know that they have extended credit to the stupendous amount of more than twenty billions of dollars to manufacturers of war material." Representative Henry Helgesen of North Dakota felt that

[1] J. E. Engstad to Knud Wefald, September 27, 1914, Wefald Papers, Minnesota Historical Society.

the United States leaned toward the Allied side simply because so many corporations "have been converted into factories for the production of munitions of war for Russia, France, and England." Thus, "Our steel companies, our powder manufacturers, and our makers of death-dealing instruments are reaping a fabulous harvest of wealth from this iniquitous traffic in human lives." [2]

Norwegians in Congress were equally offended by Wilson's foreign policy — his administration was too pro-British. Congressman Harold Knutson of Minnesota protested that Wilson issued only "faint and half-hearted protests to the various British orders in council." But with Germany the President "maintained a nagging policy that would have been creditable to a common scold." Helgesen asked Wilson, instead of pursuing a pro-British foreign policy, to "remonstrate as swiftly and as surely with Great Britain and her allies in their unwarrantable and unprecedented interference with our peaceful commerce as we should do were the offending nations on the side of the Teutonic allies." Representative Gilbert Haugen of Iowa, reminding Congress of America's neutral rights, said: "No one, so far as I know, has questioned our rights as a neutral to ship food to the people of Germany or any other country. It is agreed that that right has been denied to us by England." In short, as Congressman John Nelson of Wisconsin argued, "The President protests feebly against England and does nothing more, but he holds Germany to strict account." [3]

To avert American intervention in World War I, the Norwegians in Congress voted for the Gore-McLemore resolutions. Despite furious opposition from the Wilson administration, eight of nine Norwegians — with Senator Knute Nelson the exception — pleaded for measures refusing passports to American citizens who intended to travel on the armed ships of belligerents. As Helgesen expressed it, any American who would sail on an armed belligerent vessel "is a puny-minded egotist, who prefers to risk the embroilment of a nation of 100,000,000 people . . . rather than temporarily forgo one jot or tittle of his petty little personal right to the freedom of the seas." [4]

[2] *Congressional Record,* 53:1700, 54:831 (appendix); *Fram,* March 29, 1917.
[3] *Congressional Record,* 53:1700, 54:832 (appendix), 55:22, 79 (appendix).
[4] *Congressional Record,* 53:1700, 3465, 3720.

To the end, the Norwegians resisted a declaration of war. But on April 2, 1917, the President requested precisely that. Despite enormous pressures and charges of un-Americanism, four of the eight Norwegians in the House and Grønna in the Senate refused to countenance the joint resolution declaring war on Germany. A sixth Norwegian in Congress, Henry Helgesen of North Dakota, was unequivocally opposed to the war resolution but failed to vote because of a serious illness. A seventh, Halvor Steenorson of Minnesota, had to explain, "The authority and power of the Chief Executive of the Nation over the foreign affairs . . . of the Nation are so complete that he can and sometimes does create situations that make it the imperative duty of Congress to support him." Hence, "Congress practically has no choice, for the Nation has already been committed to a definite course."[5]

John Nelson, defying the declaration of war on Germany, assailed the industrial-munitions complex in the United States: "Long ago I took my stand for peace. I care not how much I am abused as a pacifist. I am resolved that my hands shall not be reddened nor my soul stained with the blood of my fellows, be they Germans or Americans or both — certainly not to protect the commercial rights of men who supply war materials for profit, and to one side only of the European belligerents." Grønna summed up his position in this way: "I shall . . . vote against this resolution declaring war against the Imperial Government of Germany. . . . I shall vote against war because I believe it would have been possible to maintain an honorable peace with all the nations of the earth. . . . I am opposed to war because war means destruction, misery, and poverty to the toiling millions of our country for generations to come."[6]

In North Dakota, Senator Grønna's antiwar position was endorsed by his fellow countrymen. In a survey conducted by the Works Progress Administration in North Dakota in 1939, 121 first-generation Norwegian Americans were asked whether they had supported American intervention in World War I. One hundred and five answered no, only 16, yes. One of them replied: "Did I favor America going into the first World War? No, I should say not, because I had

<hr>

[5] *Congressional Record*, 55:261, 404, 412.
[6] Wilkins, "North Dakota and the European War," 317; *Congressional Record*, 54:831 (appendix), 55:220.

the same idea then as now, only I did not dare to say it then. We were fighting for the capitalists. They thought the Allies were going to lose the war; and they wanted Uncle Sam to go over to help, so they could collect what they had loaned." Thus, "It was a money-man's war."[7]

This attitude was deeply rooted in the North Dakota Norwegian community during World War I. From the beginnings of political protest in the Middle West, the Norwegians had sensed the shaping of a corporate capitalist conspiracy. To them, exploitation was a central fact of American life; industrialists, bankers, speculators, and middlemen were suspect. To them, it was always "the interests versus the people." Albert Mork, in a letter to Senator Grønna in January, 1916, recapitulated these reactions: "Do what you can to save us from the evil designs of the armament trust, munitions grafters and the military clique." Similarly, William Anderson, a farmer of Grandin, North Dakota, applauded the efforts of both Helgesen and Grønna in resisting "the hellish designs of the bond buyers and munition manufacturers." C. O. Swenson of Northwood, North Dakota, alleged that preparedness and conscription were merely contrivances to help the "ruling class . . . launch this country into war." Writing to Grønna, L. L. Suttiff explained that the war attitudes of his friends were similar: "At a meeting of the Paradise, North Dakota, Equity Exchange, over a hundred farmers had talked the thing over and in that crowd there was not one that talked in favor of an increase in the defense effort."[8]

To conservatives in North Dakota, support of the Nonpartisan League was one thing. But to oppose participation in World War I — that was something else. The native American press, especially the largest daily newspapers, directed their criticisms at two representatives of the Norwegian community, Helgesen and Grønna. The *Grand Forks Herald* censured them for obstructing "the only course which can be pursued without repudiating the work of every patriot of the past, and without imposing on posterity a legacy of injury and shame." The *Fargo Forum* editorialized that the views of Grønna

[7] Interviews conducted in representative North Dakota counties, filed in State Historical Society of North Dakota, Bismarck; interview with John A. Haugen, June 19, 1939.

[8] Wilkins, "North Dakota and the European War," 173; *Congressional Record*, 54:592.

and Helgesen on foreign policy had "bowed the heads of many loyal North Dakotans in shame." [9]

Antiwar attitudes also plagued Minnesota conservatives. There was a resurgence of radicalism among Norwegians in the state — a resurgence that fueled the antiwar movement. Conservatives there, as in North Dakota, had long been alarmed by this radicalism. But extreme dissent in the area of American foreign policy — that was intolerable. To checkmate these sentiments, they called on a powerful Norwegian politician, Senator Knute Nelson. In April, 1917, writing to an antiwar editor, he said: "I am greatly surprised at the unpatriotic and cowardly spirit that you manifest." The reply was equally caustic: "You evidently do not know to whom you are writing. You are getting too old and cross. You are worse than the czar of Russia used to be before he was forced to abdicate." [10]

Shortly before World War I, Representative Andrew Volstead remarked to Nelson that the farmers in his district were talking "socialism and everything else." By 1916, Nicolay Grevstad, a former newspaper editor and himself increasingly conservative, was complaining to Nelson that the Norwegians seemed to be "the most unsatisfactory section of the electorate." With the spreading of the Nonpartisan League into Minnesota by 1917, they were to become even more unsatisfactory. Ole O. Sageng, a veteran Minnesota legislator, in a letter to Nelson of December, 1917, grumbled that "the political situation in Minnesota is not reassuring." He added: "To me it is discouraging. With the headway which the Non-Partisan League has made among our farmers — even a very large part of our really substantial and ordinarily cautious Scandinavian farmers have been carried away by this wholly unsound movement." By 1918, Nelson himself was willing to admit that the Nonpartisan League had "stirred up the farmers about as they were stirred up in the old times by the Populist program." [11]

By 1918, Norwegians all through the western Middle West were stirred up. In Congress, they were battling traditional foes — bankers, speculators, and corporate capitalists — as well as Wilson's policy of

[9] Wilkins, "North Dakota and the European War," 266–268, 291–294.
[10] Gieske, "The Politics of Knute Nelson," 380–385.
[11] Gieske, "The Politics of Knute Nelson," 86–90, 310–314, 445–473, 510–524, 525–530.

involvement. In both North and South Dakota, Norwegians were trying to piece together a small-scale welfare state. But whether they were La Follette Republicans, Norbeck Republicans, or Nonpartisan Leaguers, one factor remained central to most of them, in and out of Congress: they still shared the common heritage of the old country. This included a spirit of co-operation, a sense of community, concern for the public good, and sympathy for the have-nots. It also set a common goal for the majority: America should become a veritable co-operative commonwealth.

But this ideal could not be realized. It was too dependent on the values and traditions of rural Norway. The process of Americanization eroded. Some of the old-country outlook was to persist into the 1920's and 1930's — in the Congressional farm bloc, the La Follette Republicans in Wisconsin, the Norbeck Republicans in South Dakota, the Nonpartisan League in North Dakota, and the Farmer-Labor party in Minnesota. By the 1940's and 1950's, the process of assimilation was largely completed. But not before Floyd B. Olson and the Farmer-Labor party had come to dominate Minnesota politics during the 1930's. Not before Farmer-Laborites, led by Scandinavians like Olson, K. K. Solberg, Elmer Benson, H. H. Peterson, and Hjalmar Peterson, radicalized state politics and wrote, as George H. Mayer says, the most radical platform "ever drawn up by an American party actually holding political power." Not before Governor Olson stirred up the Middle Western Norwegians with this exhortation at the Minnesota Farmer-Labor convention in 1934: "Now I am frank to say that I am not a liberal. . . . I am what I want to be — I am a radical. . . . What is the ultimate we are seeking? . . . The ultimate is a Cooperative Commonwealth."[12]

[12] Mayer, *The Political Career of Floyd B. Olson*, 165–183; William E. Leuchtenburg, *Franklin D. Roosevelt and the New Deal*, 96 (New York, 1963).

APPENDIX

Reform Votes in Congress

Year	*Bill or Amendment*	*Norwegians in Congress*	*Yes*	*No*	*NV*
1905	Esch-Townshend bill, a measure setting limits on court review of ICC decisions, in House	Haugen, Iowa	*		
		Steenorson, Minn.	*		
		Volstead, Minn.	*		
1906	Senate amendment to Hepburn bill prohibiting carriers from issuing free tickets or passes	Nelson, Minn.	*		
1906	Senate amendment to Hepburn bill adding physical valuations	Nelson, Minn.		*	
1906	Hepburn bill in House allowing ICC to fix railroad rates	Haugen, Iowa	*		
		Steenorson, Minn.	*		
		Volstead, Minn.	*		
		Grønna, N. D.			*
1906	Hepburn bill in Senate	Nelson, Minn.	*		

NOTE. *Congressional Record*, 39:2205, 40:2773, 6455, 6809, 7088, 9075, 9084, 44:4120, 4440, 45:5567, 6033, 7199, 7375, 50:1386, 3773, 4617, 5128, 5129, 51:1230, 1914, 5108, 9911, 9912, 13319, 14610, 16170, 16344, 52:1483, 53:2035, 7271, 10916, 12313, 13608, 13655.

Year	Bill or Amendment	Norwegians in Congress	Yes	No	NV
1906	Pure food and drug bill in House	Haugen, Iowa	✿		
		Steenorson, Minn.	✿		
		Volstead, Minn.	✿		
		Grønna, N. D.			✿
1906	Pure food and drug bill in Senate	Nelson, Minn.	✿		
1909	Joint resolution for income tax in House	Haugen, Iowa	✿		
		Grønna, N. D.	✿		
		Nelson, Wis.	✿		
		Steenorson, Minn.	✿		
		Volstead, Minn.	✿		
1909	Joint resolution for income tax in Senate	Nelson, Minn.	✿		
		Johnson, N. D.	✿		
1910	Senate amendment to Mann-Elkins bill allowing for physical valuations of railroads	Nelson, Minn.	✿		
1910	Senate vote allowing ICC to suspend new rail rates	Nelson, Minn.	✿		
1910	Mann-Elkins bill in House giving ICC power to suspend new rail rates pending a court decision	Haugen, Iowa	✿		
		Grønna, N. D.	✿		
		Nelson, Wis.	✿		
		Steenorson, Minn.	✿		
		Volstead, Minn.	✿		
1910	Mann-Elkins bill in Senate	Nelson, Minn.	✿		
1913	Underwood bill revising the tariff downward in House	Haugen, Iowa		✿	
		Nelson, Wis.		✿	
		Steenorson, Minn.		✿	
		Volstead, Minn.		✿	
		Anderson, Minn.		✿	
		Helgesen, N. D.		✿	
1913	Underwood bill in Senate	Nelson, Minn.		✿	
		Grønna, N. D.		✿	
1913	Tax amendment to Underwood bill in Senate	Nelson, Minn.	✿		
		Grønna, N. D.			✿
1913	House amendment to Federal Reserve System bill prohibiting an officer or director of one bank, etc., from becoming an officer or director of another bank	Anderson, Minn.	✿		
		Haugen, Iowa	✿		
		Helgesen, N. D.	✿		
		Nelson, Wis.	✿		
		Steenorson, Minn.	✿		
		Volstead, Minn.	✿		
1913	Federal Reserve bill in House creating a government-con-	Haugen, Iowa	✿		
		Helgesen, N. D.	✿		

Year	Bill or Amendment	Norwegians in Congress	Yes	No	NV
	trolled decentralized banking system	Nelson, Wis.	✿		
		Steenorson, Minn.		✿	
		Volstead, Minn.		✿	
		Anderson, Minn.		✿	
1913	Federal Reserve bill in Senate	Nelson, Minn.		✿	
		Grønna, N. D.		✿	
1914	Rayburn bill in House giving ICC authority over the issuance of new securities by railroads	Anderson, Minn.	✿		
		Haugen, Iowa	✿		
		Helgesen, N. D.	✿		
		Steenorson, Minn.	✿		
		Volstead, Minn.	✿		
		Nelson, Wis.	✿		
1914	Senate amendment putting teeth back into Senate version of Clayton antitrust bill	Nelson, Minn.	✿		
		Grønna, N. D.	✿		
1914	Passage in House of Clayton antitrust bill supplementing Sherman Antitrust Act	Helgesen, N. D.		✿	
		Volstead, Minn.		✿	
		Steenorson, Minn.		✿	
		Nelson, Wis.		✿	
		Anderson, Minn.			✿
		Haugen, Iowa			✿
1914	Clayton bill in Senate	Nelson, Minn.		✿	
		Grønna, N. D.			✿
1914	Federal Trade Commission bill in Senate	Nelson, Minn.		✿	
		Grønna, N.D.			✿
1915	Woman suffrage amendment in House	Anderson, Minn.	✿		
		Haugen, Iowa	✿		
		Nelson, Wis.	✿		
		Helgesen, N. D.	✿		
		Volstead, Minn.	✿		
		Steenorson, Minn.	✿		
1915	Woman suffrage amendment in Senate	Nelson, Minn.	✿		
		Grønna, N. D.	✿		
1916	Warehouse bill in House authorizing licensed and bonded warehouses to assist farmers in financing crops	Anderson, Minn.	✿		
		Haugen, Iowa	✿		
		Helgesen, N. D.	✿		
		Nelson, Wis.	✿		
		Steenorson, Minn.	✿		
		Volstead, Minn.	✿		
1916	Child labor bill in House barring from interstate commerce products of child labor	Anderson, Minn.	✿		
		Helgesen, N. D.	✿		
		Nelson, Wis.	✿		
		Steenorson, Minn.	✿		

Year	Bill or Amendment	Norwegians in Congress	Yes	No	NV
	Child labor bill (*continued*)	Volstead, Minn.	✻		
		Haugen, Iowa			✻
1916	Child labor bill in Senate	Nelson, Minn.	✻		
		Grønna, N. D.	✻		
1916	Adamson bill in House specifying an eight-hour work day on railroads operating in interstate commerce	Haugen, Iowa	✻		
		Helgesen, N. D.	✻		
		Nelson, Wis.	✻		
		Volstead, Minn.	✻		
		Steenorson, Minn.	✻		
		Anderson, Minn.			✻
1916	Adamson bill in Senate	Nelson, Minn.		✻	
		Grønna, N. D.		✻	
1916	Workmen's compensation bill in House providing compensation for injuries to federal employees	Anderson, Minn.	✻		
		Helgesen, N. D.	✻		
		Nelson, Wis.	✻		
		Volstead, Minn.	✻		
		Steenorson, Minn.	✻		
		Haugen, Iowa			✻

BIBLIOGRAPHY AND INDEX

LIST OF SYMBOLS

LLC	Library, Luther College, Decorah, Iowa
NDHS	State Historical Society of North Dakota
NAHA	Norwegian-American Historical Association archives, Northfield
MHS	Minnesota Historical Society, St. Paul
SDHS	South Dakota Historical Society, Pierre
WHS	State Historical Society of Wisconsin, Madison

Bibliography

ARCHIVES AND MANUSCRIPTS

Davidson, James O., papers. WHS.
Ethnic group interviews. NDHS.
Grevstad, Nicolay A., papers. NAHA.
Haugen, Nils P., papers. WHS.
Lee, Andrew E., papers. SDHS.
Nelson, Knute, papers. MHS.
Wefald, Knud, papers. MHS.

GOVERNMENT PUBLICATIONS

State of Minnesota, *Legislative Manual*, 1893, 1901, 1917, 1931.
State of North Dakota, *Legislative Manual*, 1907, 1913, 1919.
State of South Dakota, *Legislative Manual*, 1917, 1919, 1925.
United States Census, 1901, *Population.*
United States Census, 1913, *Population*, v. 2, 3.
Congressional Record, v. 21–55 (1890–1917).

NEWSPAPERS

Afholds-Basunen (Hillsboro, N. D.), 1890–1896. Weekly. Incomplete file, LLC.
    Populist-Prohibitionist.
Dell Rapids Tribune (Dell Rapids, S. D.), 1892–1906. Weekly. SDHS. Republi-
    can.

Drayton Echo (Drayton, N. D.), 1889–1896. Weekly. NDHS. Republican.
Faribault Republican (Faribault, Minn.), 1892–1900. Weekly. MHS. Republican.
Fergus Falls Ugeblad (Fergus Falls, Minn.), 1904–1912. Weekly. Incomplete file, LLC. Populist-Democratic.
Fram (Fargo, N. D.), 1902–1917. Weekly. Incomplete file, LLC. Republican.
Fremad (Sioux Falls, S. D.), 1896–1916. Weekly. Incomplete file, LLC. Populist-Democratic.
Gary Inter-State (Gary, S. D.), 1892–1902. Weekly. SDHS. Republican.
Hillsboro Banner (Hillsboro, N. D.), 1912–1917. Weekly. NDHS. Republican.
Martin County Sentinel (Fairmont, Minn.), 1890–1894. Daily, semiweekly, weekly. NDHS. Republican.
Mayville Tribune (Mayville, N. D.), 1889–1917. Weekly. NDHS. Republican.
Minneapolis Tribune, 1892–1917. Daily. MHS. Republican.
Nordvesten (St. Paul), 1892, 1900–1904. Weekly. Incomplete file, LLC. Republican.
Norman County Herald (Ada, Minn.), 1890–1896, 1917. Weekly. MHS. Populist-Democratic.
North (Minneapolis), 1889–1894. Weekly. Incomplete file. MHS. Independent.
Nye Normanden (Minneapolis), 1896–1904. Weekly. Incomplete file, LLC. Populist-Democratic.
Rock County Herald (Luverne, Minn.), 1892–1898. Weekly. MHS. Republican.
St. Paul Dispatch, 1892–1896, 1917. Daily. MHS. Republican.
St. Paul Pioneer Press, 1892–1896, 1917. (Title varies.) Daily. MHS. Republican.
Sioux Falls Posten (Sioux Falls, S. D.), 1908–1915. Weekly. Incomplete file, LLC. Republican.
Skandinaven (Chicago), 1890–1917. Daily, semiweekly. Incomplete file, LLC. Republican.
Statstidende (Hillsboro, N. D.), 1897–1904. Weekly. Incomplete file, LLC. Republican.
Syd Dakota Ekko (Sioux Falls, S. D.), 1893–1906. Weekly. Incomplete file, LLC. Republican.

BOOKS

Andersen, Arlow William, *The Immigrant Takes His Stand: The Norwegian-American Press and Public Affairs, 1847–1872* (Northfield, 1953).
Anderson, Rasmus B., *Life Story of Rasmus B. Anderson* (Madison, 1917.)
Bergmann, Leola Nelson, *Americans from Norway* (New York, 1950).
Blegen, Theodore C., ed., *Frontier Parsonage: The Letters of Olaus Fredrik Duus* (Northfield, 1947).
———, ed., *Land of Their Choice: The Immigrants Write Home* (Minneapolis, 1955).
———, *Norwegian Migration to America, 1825–1860* (Northfield, 1931).
———, *Norwegian Migration to America: The American Transition* (Northfield, 1940).
———, ed., and Martin B. Ruud, trans., *Norwegian Emigrant Songs and Ballads* (Minneapolis, 1936).
Bojer, Johan, *The Emigrants* (New York, 1937).
Bruce, Andrew A., *Non-Partisan League* (New York, 1921).
Curti, Merle, *The Making of an American Community: A Case Study of Democracy in a Frontier County* (Stanford, Calif., 1959).
Dalthorp, Charles J., ed., *South Dakota's Governors* (Sioux Falls, S. D., 1953).

Degler, Carl N., *Out of Our Past* (New York, 1959).
Democratic Folk Movements in Scandinavia (Minneapolis, 1951).
Dorfman, Joseph, *Thorstein Veblen and His America* (New York, 1934).
Eckstein, Harry, *Division and Cohesion in Democracy: A Study of Norway* (Princeton, 1966).
Fite, Gilbert C., *Peter Norbeck: Prairie Statesman* (Columbia, Mo., 1948).
Flom, George T., *A History of Norwegian Immigration to the United States* (Iowa City, Iowa, 1909).
Gaston, Herbert E., *The Nonpartisan League* (New York, 1920).
Gjerset, Knut, *History of the Norwegian People*, vol. 2 (New York, 1915).
Goldman, Eric F., *Rendezvous with Destiny* (New York, 1952).
Grimley, O. B., *The New Norway: A People with the Spirit of Cooperation* (Oslo, 1937).
Handlin, Oscar, *The Uprooted* (New York, 1951).
Hicks, John D., and Theodore Saloutos, *Agricultural Discontent in the Middle West, 1900–1939* (Madison, 1951).
Hofstadter, Richard, *The Age of Reform: From Bryan to F.D.R.* (New York, 1955).
Jones, Maldwyn Allen, *American Immigration* (Chicago, 1960).
Knaplund, Paul, *Moorings Old and New: Entries in an Immigrant's Log* (Madison, 1963).
Koht, Halvdan, and Sigmund Skard, *The Voice of Norway* (Morningside Heights, N.Y., 1944).
Larsen, Karen, *A History of Norway* (Princeton, 1948).
Larson, Agnes M., *John A. Johnson: An Uncommon American* (Northfield, 1969).
Larson, Laurence M., *The Changing West and Other Essays* (Northfield, 1937).
Leuchtenburg, William E., *Franklin D. Roosevelt and the New Deal* (New York, 1963).
Link, Arthur S., *Woodrow Wilson and the Progressive Era* (New York, 1954).
Maxwell, Robert, *La Follette and the Rise of the Progressives in Wisconsin* (Madison, 1956).
Mayer, George H., *The Political Career of Floyd B. Olson* (Minneapolis, 1951).
Miller, William, ed., *Men in Business* (New York, 1952).
Morlan, Robert L., *Political Prairie Fire* (Minneapolis, 1955).
Mowry, George E., *The Era of Theodore Roosevelt, 1900–1912* (New York, 1958).
Munch, Peter A., *A Study of Cultural Change: Rural-Urban Conflicts in Norway* (Oslo, 1956).
Nordskog, John Eric, *Social Reform in Norway* (Los Angeles, 1935).
Norlie, Olaf M., *History of the Norwegian People in America* (Minneapolis, 1925).
Nye, Russell B., *Midwestern Progressive Politics* (East Lansing, Mich., 1959).
Odland, Martin W., *The Life of Knute Nelson* (Minneapolis, 1926).
Qualey, Carlton C., *Norwegian Settlement in the United States* (Northfield, 1938).
Robinson, Elwyn R., *History of North Dakota* (Lincoln, Neb., 1966).
Rodnick, David, *The Norwegians: A Study in National Culture* (Washington, D. C., 1955).
Schell, Herbert, *History of South Dakota* (Lincoln, Neb., 1961).
Stephenson, George, *John Lind of Minnesota* (Minneapolis, 1935).
Troeltsch, Ernst, *Protestantism and Progress* (Boston, 1912).
Warner, W. Lloyd, *Democracy in Jonesville: A Study of Quality and Inequality* (New York, 1949).

ARTICLES

Dieserud, Juul, "Norwegians in the Public and Political Life of the United States," in *Scandinavia*, 1:49–58 (March, 1924).
Frederickson, George M., "Thorstein Veblen: The Last Viking," in *American Quarterly*, 11:404–406 (Fall, 1959).
Gjerset, Knut, "A Norwegian-American Landnamsman: Ole S. Gjerset," in Norwegian-American Historical Association, *Studies and Records*, 3:94 (1928).
Haugen, Einar, "Norwegian Migration to America," in *Norwegian-American Studies and Records*, 18:10 (1954).
Hicks, John D., "The People's Party in Minnesota," in *Minnesota History Bulletin*, 5:531–560 (November, 1924).
Løvoll, Odd Sverre, "The Norwegian Press in North Dakota," in *Norwegian-American Studies*, 24:78–101 (Northfield, 1970).
Milgram, Stanley, "Nationality and Conformity," in *Scientific American*, 205:50 (December, 1961).
Munch, Peter A., "Gard: The Norwegian Farm," in *Rural Sociology*, 12:357 (December, 1947).
————, "Segregation and Assimilation of Norwegian Settlements in Wisconsin," in *Norwegian-American Studies and Records*, 18:125 (1954).
Naftalin, Arthur, "The Tradition of Protest and the Roots of the Farmer-Labor Party," in *Minnesota History*, 35:53–63 (June, 1956).
Vecoli, Rudolph J., "*Contadini* in Chicago: A Critique of *The Uprooted*," in *Journal of American History*, 1:404–407 (December, 1964).
Vogt, Evon Z., Jr., "Social Stratification in the Rural Middlewest: A Structural Analysis," in *Rural Sociology*, 12:365 (December, 1947).
Wyman, Roger E., "Insurgency in Minnesota: The Defeat of James A. Tawney in 1910," in *Minnesota History*, 40:317–329 (Fall, 1967).

UNPUBLISHED STUDIES

Barone, Michael, "The Social Basis of Urban Politics: Minneapolis and St. Paul, 1890–1905." Honors thesis, Harvard University, 1965.
Chrislock, Carl H., "The Politics of Protest in Minnesota, 1890–1901: From Populism to Progressivism." Doctoral dissertation, University of Minnesota, 1954.
Gieske, Millard L., "The Politics of Knute Nelson, 1912–1920." Doctoral dissertation, University of Minnesota, 1965.
Gunderson, Dora J., "The Settlement of Clay County, Minnesota, 1870–1900." Master's thesis, University of Minnesota, 1929.
Olson, Michael L., "Scandinavian Immigrant Farmer Participation in Agrarian Unrest in Western Minnesota." Honors thesis, St. Olaf College, 1965.
Phillips, William W., "The Growth of a Progressive: Asle J. Gronna." Master's thesis, University of North Dakota, 1952.
Putnam, Jackson K., "The Socialist Party of North Dakota, 1902–1918." Master's thesis, University of North Dakota, 1956.
Wilkins, Robert P., "North Dakota and the European War." Doctoral dissertation, University of West Virginia, 1954.

Index